FAULKNER'S

Light in August

Title page of the original edition. Reproduced
with the kind permission of Maurice Edgar Coindreau, who translated *Light in August* into French.

LIGHT IN AUGUST

WILLIAM FAULKNER

HARRISON SMITH & ROBERT HAAS

FAULKNER'S

Light in August

BY

François Pitavy

REVISED AND ENLARGED EDITION

TRANSLATED BY

GILLIAN E. COOK

WITH THE COLLABORATION OF THE AUTHOR

1982

Indiana University Press

BLOOMINGTON / LONDON

THE AUTHOR WOULD LIKE TO THANK Mrs. Jill Faulkner Summers for permitting him to use and quote the manuscript of *Light in August* and reproduce a page of it, and to quote one of Faulkner's unpublished texts, now in trust with the Alderman Library at the University of Virginia. He would also like to thank the Humanities Research Center of the University of Texas and to express his gratitude to Mr. Linton R. Massey.

CONTENTS

CONTENTS

FAULKNER'S

Light in August

THE TEXT OF *Light in August* used for this study is the first edition published by Smith & Haas. The 1967 Random House edition and the 1968 Modern Library College Edition (with an excellent introduction by Cleanth Brooks) may also be referred to, as both are reproductions of the original. The earlier Modern Library edition (1950), which for some years contained a mediocre introduction by Richard Rovere, is not recommended: the pagination differs from that of the first edition and there are too many errors, and even omissions.

Apart from some minor inaccuracies which the reader will easily correct for himself, the first edition has two errors:

P. 240, l. 8: for "He once cursed Him," read "He once cursed him"; it is true to both the manuscript and the typescript, and it invalidates any heretical commentaries;

P. 340, l. 1: for "Jefferson," read "Mottstown," as indeed the sense of the text suggests. In the manuscript there is the following sentence: "And then when suppertime came they did something else they hadn't ever done before since they came to Mottstown that anybody could remember." But the word Mottstown is so badly written that it is understandable that Faulkner should have made a careless mistake in typing out this passage.

1

Overview and Composition

BETWEEN THE WRITING OF *The Sound and the Fury* in 1928 and the completion of *Absalom, Absalom!* in 1936, William Faulkner's literary output was remarkably prolific. In the space of less than ten years he wrote and published six novels and two volumes of short stories which rank among his finest work, and he revised several poems for publication in a collection. *Light in August*, with *The Sound and the Fury* and *Absalom, Absalom!*, is one of the masterpieces issuing from this period of extraordinary inspiration and craftsmanship.

The true dimension of the novel has been underestimated sufficiently often, especially in the first few years after its publication,[1] to make the clearing up of a few misconceptions useful. Before launching into a study of the several aspects of this novel and saying what it is about, it may be useful also to circumscribe the ground by stating what it is not.

Some of the early reviewers—and also later readers and even critics—were somewhat disturbed by the exposé of people's attitudes toward miscegenation (and one of the most frequent misreadings was, and occasionally still is, considering Joe Christmas as definitely of mixed blood), and by what they deemed the author's unpleasant insistence on violence or such sordid aspects of life as prostitution, nymphomania, lynching, and castration (and by the way,

Christmas is not lynched, but killed by Percy Grimm). As a result, *Light in August* was sometimes classed—and misunderstood—with *Sanctuary*, which had been something of a scandal on its publication, eighteen months earlier. However, *Light in August* is definitely not a novel of "sex and violence": by limiting himself to its sensational aspect, the reader will receive a totally mistaken idea of the novel's import. Faulkner never uses sensationalism for its own sake—and this applies equally to *Sanctuary*. It is for him nothing more than one of the tools available to the writer wishing to picture the discovery of evil, or the tragedy of a man incapable of affirming his identity except through violence. Faulkner himself has frequently, and unequivocally, explained his feeling on this point; for instance, at the University of Virginia he said:

> If [the writer] is creating characters which are flesh-and-blood people, are believable, and are honest and true, then he can use sensationalism if he thinks that's an effective way to tell his story. But if he's writing just for sensationalism, then he has betrayed his vocation, and he deserves to suffer from it. That is, sensationalism is in a way an incidental tool, that he might use sensationalism as a carpenter picks up another hammer to drive a nail. But he doesn't—the carpenter don't build a house just to drive nails. He drives nails to build a house.[2]

It would be equally untrue to say that *Light in August* is a novel about the South. It is no part of Faulkner's purpose to report on the local news of a small Mississippi town, nor to describe the life of its inhabitants. There are no "realistic" descriptions in this book, and no political or sociological remarks as such. Faulkner's own imaginary county of Yoknapatawpha, of which he rightly claimed to be the sole owner and proprietor, will never match Lafayette County in Mississippi: and while the latter offers the sociologist and historian an area for observation, the former furnishes Faulkner with an epitome of the universe, the stage on which the human comedy is played out: "Beginning with *Sartoris* I discovered that my own little postage stamp of native soil was worth writing about and that I would never live long enough to exhaust it, and by sublimating the actual into apocryphal I would have complete liberty to use whatever talent I might have to its absolute top. It opened up a gold mine of other peoples, so I created a cosmos of my own."[3] It is probably the ambition to merge the two together which makes *Intruder in the Dust* a partial failure. Yoknapatawpha County only appears to be real because Faulkner has used in its creation the materials he found at hand, the environment he knew best, to use a word he liked: "A writer is trying to create believable people in credible moving situations in the most moving way he can. Obviously he must use as one of his tools the environment which he knows."[4]

In all probability he took the idea for the story of Joe Christmas from a news item well known in Oxford, Mississippi. In *Old Times in the Faulkner Country*,[5] John B. Cullen tells how, on the morning of September 8, 1908, a Negro, Nelse Patton, went to deliver to one Mrs. McMillan, a white woman living outside the town, a letter from her husband, who was in prison. The Negro then killed the woman, cutting her throat with his razor and almost completely severing her head (chapter 16 of *Sanctuary* begins with an account of a very similar murder). The murderer was caught shortly afterward thanks to John B. Cullen himself, then only fourteen, armed with his hunting rifle. Soon hundreds of people gathered outside the prison, and a former senator, W. V. Sullivan, urged the crowd to lynch the murderer. The next day, he told reporters: "I led the mob that lynched Nelse Patton and I am proud of it." The crowd spent part of the night breaking through the wall around the cells, inside the prison, the sheriff having gone off with the keys for fear of having them taken from him by force. Nelse Patton seriously injured three men with a shovel before he was brought down by a pistol shot. His body was dragged outside, where he was castrated, scalped, and hanged. John Cullen remarks: "Nelse Patton's crime and the lynching of Nelse are more widely known than anything else of this kind that ever happened in Lafayette County. William Faulkner was eleven years old at the time, and since he has spent most of his life in this community, he must have heard numerous stories about the Patton case." The similarities to, but, even more, the differences from the story of Joe Christmas stand out. Faulkner may have made use of the news item, but if he did, he preserved only some obvious and unimportant details of the original. The characters of Joanna and Joe are complete innovations, indeed inventions, the latter offering a classic example of alienation in his life and above all in the doubts clouding his birth and his blood. "[Faulkner] changes characters as much as Pat Stamper and Flem Snopes would change horses before they traded them," John Cullen explains humorously.[6] As Louis D. Rubin says,

> Joe Christmas is not the "average" Southern Negro or even the portrait of a typical victim of a lynch mob . . . . He is an exaggeration, a tragic hero . . . . By pursuing Joe Christmas' human dimensions to their ultimate proportions Faulkner is able to dramatize that humanness, to show it to us clean, unflawed by compromise or qualification. He shows us . . . what it means to be a human being, and we recognize in this pervert, this murderer, this criminal, what is also present in ourselves.[7]

Christmas is not primarily a Southerner: more importantly, he is a man the tragedy of whose destiny is intensified because of his environment and those experiences in the South which have scarred him.

It is for this reason that the title itself has far more than a local, limited significance. With *The Portable Faulkner*, Malcolm Cowley became the first to try to put a geographical boundary to the meaning of the title, so initiating an interpretation which has all too often been accepted: "the title of the novel has nothing to do with August sunlight; it refers to Lena Grove and her baby. In the Mississippi backwoods, it is sometimes said of a pregnant woman, but more often of a mare or a cow, that she will be *light* in August or September."[8] Faulkner has always rejected this interpretation as false: "It refers to a texture of the light in August in my country, in a spell of two or three cool days we call 'Blackberry Winter.' It's the light. I had never heard that business of after the cow drops the calf she's light in August."[9] He has explained that in his country the August light seemed for a few days in the middle of the month to emanate from Grecian antiquity, from civilizations before Christianity, and that Lena Grove suggested for him that same quality, that pagan luminosity.[10] Thus even if such a phrase does exist in Mississippi (and Faulkner was surely in a position to know of it), by applying it to *Light in August* the real dimension of the novel is lost.

However, the critical reservations felt about the book are caused by its form more than by its themes or some blatant details, and this has more than once prevented a ready appreciation of the novel. *Light in August* may be a long novel, Faulkner's longest, in fact, apart from *A Fable* and *The Mansion,* but it is easier to read than the other "greats" of the period: the events are easily followed, and Faulkner is not, apparently at least, experimenting with any new or striking novelistic form. Yet in spite of appearances, it is a relatively complex novel.

To begin with, there is a large number of characters, nearly seventy in all, more than in *The Sound and the Fury,* about thirty more than in *As I Lay Dying,* and almost twice as many as in *Absalom, Absalom!* Admittedly, there are fewer principals than in the other three novels, yet they do not appear to be closely interrelated. Sometimes the numerous secondary characters (though present in nothing approaching the proliferation of the last novels) give an impression of diffusion. Some, like Doc Hines or Brown, are suddenly given an importance out of all proportion to their role in the plot. Others, like Percy Grimm or the furniture dealer, curiously appear at the end of the novel.

The plot itself is complex and puzzling. At times, as in the story of Joe's life, it is extremely concentrated and has a remarkable unity. At other times it seems to leap erratically from one character to another in loosely related scenes. One cannot even say that there is one main plot. In fact, without taking into account any of the minor offshoots, there are three, each with its protagonist: Lena Grove, Joe Christmas, and Gail Hightower. The links between these three characters seem frail or nonexistent: Hightower delivers Lena's baby, but he does not know her; Joe and Hightower only meet *in extremis*, and Hightower's attempt to save Joe is futile, not to say risible; Lena and Joe never meet, and it can be assumed that Joe does not even know of Lena's existence. Some people see Lena Grove and Joe Christmas as opposite poles, and this is true, but it leaves Hightower out of account. It seems then that those critics who condemn the work for its lack of unity may have some reason for their reproof, so persistently does the human mind seek to bring order out of chaos and find an immediately recognizable design in every work of art. While acknowledging the rich substance of the novel and its immediate rendering of life, Irving Howe writes: "The most stringent criticism—too stringent I should think—to be made of *Light in August* is that Faulkner's clumsiness in transitional stitching and narrative preparation . . . reduces the book to a series of brilliant tableaux."[11] In his introduction to the 1950 Modern Library edition of the novel, Richard H. Rovere asserts: "It is looser in form and structure than any of the others and among the most implausible in plot." Such judgments, while not necessarily resulting from a superficial reading, solely on the level of plot, show perhaps a certain regret at not being able to discover a traditional structure in an apparently uncomplicated work, with no striking innovations in technique, and one moreover which belongs neither to the saga nor the picaresque type, but which is on the contrary sufficiently condensed in time and space (at least in the action in the present) to have an easily distinguishable principle of unity. Richard P. Adams sums up this feeling of unease in relation to the novel's form: "Critics have had a great deal of trouble in efforts to demonstrate any general unity in *Light in August,* and have sometimes concluded that it is an inferior book." [12]

As a result, many readers and critics concentrate on one prominent theme or symbol—acceptance or rejection of the values of the community, the alienation of Man, the burden of Calvinism, the Christian symbolism, Man's relationship with nature—in an effort to bring to the surface some hidden structural design which would give the novel unity. Even though such readings may be complementary rather than contradictory, the diversity of explanations is a little disquieting. Moreover, concentration on one theme means that the others are partially neglected, whereas one of the many glories of *Light in August* is the richness and variety of its themes. Even if they can be arranged along lines of force as between the poles of a magnetic field, the resulting simplicity is misleading, as these themes are not stated in abstract, but developed through the vital unpredictability of the characters whose ambiguities they share. Furthermore, Faulkner's irony frequently undermines any interpretations the reader may think he has found.

The following chapters will attempt to show that in spite of minor faults, *Light in August* is a solidly designed work, and that it does mark the beginning of a search for a new form—a contrapuntal structure—which reaches an extreme development, possibly an impasse, in *The Wild*

Palms: in and through this structure, Faulkner's intentions may be seen. On the surface level, *Light in August* reads like a very good story and even, for a few chapters, like a cleverly told detective story (a kind of narrative Faulkner obviously relished, as it both masked and perfectly served his real ends: many of his works are genuine inquiries which draw the reader further and further into the gradually revealed consciousness of his characters). But more profoundly, it is a parable of the human condition, to the extent that Malraux's famous definition of *Sanctuary* as the intrusion of Greek tragedy into the detective novel might equally apply to *Light in August*. However, even such a comparison is misleading, precisely in view of the use of counterpoint. Although Joe Christmas's life story occupies a prominent place, the novel is concerned not only with man's doomed rebellion against himself and the whole of mankind but also with the endurance and the persistence of mankind: more accurately, as appears from the structure, these themes achieve a proper resonance only through their confrontation—as is the case of the two interlocked and inseparable stories which make up *The Wild Palms.* Thus, *Light in August* has a greater human dimension than *Sanctuary* (it is obvious even in the far more individualized characters) because of the scope offered by Lena Grove and by Hightower's position as a link between the two poles. This latter, the moral center of the work, as is Horace Benbow in *Sanctuary,* is in the end, and unlike Benbow, neither discouraged nor conquered. Thanks to him and Lena, and in spite of the Faulknerian irony and ambiguities, *Light in August* does not close upon a pessimistic vision of the human state: this is a work which remains open, be it only to the many possibilities of interpretation.

The manuscript of *Light in August* and the typescript setting copy are both in trust with the Alderman Library at the University of Virginia. The 188-page manuscript is complete. In it, Faulkner's writing is regular, but minute, compressed, and often almost indecipherable, because of the way certain groups of letters, usually at the end of a word, are more like a private shorthand than recognizable characters. The flyleaf, where the original title, *Dark House*, is crossed out in favor of the final one, gives the following information: "Oxford, Mississippi/17 August, 1931." The last page is inscribed "Oxford, Miss./19 Feb. 1932."

As far as one can judge from a study of the manuscript, Faulkner must have felt some indecision during the first months of composition. Changes in pagination and in chapter numbers suggest a degree of uncertainty over the order of several chapters, and particularly show that the present chapter 3, the description of Hightower in his study, originally opened the book. When examining page 24 of the manuscript, the first page of this chapter, one discovers that the 2 and the 4 are in slightly different ink and writing, and that the chapter number III was originally I. The University of Texas at Austin has two and a half pages of manuscript from an inferior and probably earlier version of this opening with Hightower, but there the novel is already called *Light in August*. Also at Austin, there is an untitled page bearing the number 1, with a few manuscript lines describing the arrest of a man called Brown. During nearly the whole first half of the manuscript there are signs of one, sometimes two, and perhaps three, intermediary versions in the form of passages cut out and pasted onto the pages of the final text. Moreover, a first version of the beginning in the salesman's dummy issued by Harrison Smith in 1932 (most probably early in the year, as Smith's merger with Robert Haas is announced as of March 26, 1932, in *The Publishers' Weekly*), as we shall see later, contains interesting variations from the final text—which is closer to the manuscript than to the dummy. Now as far as can be judged, it seems likely that Faulkner sent the dummy to the editor in the late fall of 1931 (Harrison Smith's break with Jonathan Cape came on November 14, 1931, according to *The Publishers' Weekly*). The manuscript of the first chapter must therefore have been revised to the form in which it now stands after the text had been sent in for the salesman's dummy, that is to say, a few months after work had begun on the novel. These few points (a study of the writing provides no certainty in this case) suggest that, as the composition of *Light in August* progressed, Faulkner began to feel that the opening of his novel no longer fitted in with the shape of the work as it was now developing, and that it was in fact inadequate to his conception of it and demanded revision—which proved to be several. He must then have spent proportionately more time on the first chapters than on the rest of the novel. An article in the "Talk of the Town" section of *The New Yorker* of November 28, 1931, corroborates this impression, if one dare trust its accuracy (it contains several biographical errors): "[William Faulkner] spends most of his days alone, working on his next novel, which is to be called *Light in August*. It's about a quarter done." [13] After about three months' work on a novel which would be completed in six, Faulkner had apparently only a quarter finished; to complete the remainder of such a long and richly conceived work in such a short time shows the speed of composition once the initial difficulties were overcome. A partly unpublished text reproduced below reveals that the novel was written with great deliberation and relative speed. This is confirmed yet again in a letter received by Faulkner's literary agent, Ben Wasson, on January 26, 1932, three weeks before the completion of the manuscript: in this letter, Faulkner explains that he has not yet started to type the novel as its composition was going too well to be interrupted. [14]

The typescript setting copy is incomplete, breaking off in chapter 19 (the remainder is in the Faulkner Collection at the Univesity of Texas). There are many differences between it and the manuscript, but these affect neither the structure nor the import of the work: they consist of words, sentences, even paragraphs either deleted, added, or altered. Several examples will be mentioned in the course of this study. The book was published on October 9, 1932 by Smith & Haas. The dust jacket and flyleaf were decorated with symbolic rays of light.

In a fine and carefully worded text which he apparently wrote toward the end of 1932 or the beginning of 1933, Faulkner explains that after *The Sound and the Fury* he could not recapture "that ecstasy, that eager and joyous faith and anticipation of surprise which the yet unmarred sheet beneath [his] hand held inviolate and unfailing, waiting for release," which he had experienced during the writing of his first masterpiece: [15]

> It was not there in As I Lay Dying . . . . I waited almost two years, then I began Light in August, knowing no more about it than a young woman, pregnant, walking along a strange country road. I thought, I will recapture it now, since I know no more about this book than I did about The Sound and the Fury when I sat down before the first blank page.
>
> It did not return. The written pages grew in number. The story was going pretty well: I would sit down to it each morning without reluctance yet without that anticipation and that joy which alone ever made writing pleasure to me. The book was almost finished before I acquiesced to the fact that it would not recur, since I was now aware before each word was written down just what the people would do, since now I was deliberately choosing among possibilities and probabilities of behavior and weighing and measuring each choice by the scale of the Jameses and Conrads and Balzacs. I knew that I had read too much, that I had reached that stage which all young writers must pass through, in which he believes that he had learned too much about his trade. I received a copy of the printed book and found that I didn't even want to see what kind of jacket Smith had put on it.

Even though he could not recapture the ecstasy of writing, Faulkner admits that in *Light in August* he had complete control over his materials and was master of his profession.

2

Structure and Technique

IN *LIGHT IN AUGUST,* Faulkner set himself a difficult task by deciding to build his story around three separate but connected plots, each of which requires individual handling to avoid confusion: he had to fit them into the time scheme of the story by dividing and rearranging them according to a precise design which it is very important to define. Moreover, the time of the novel is not limited to the present, consisting of the ten days between the murders of Joanna Burden and Joe Christmas: the account of these ten days is constantly interrrupted by flashbacks which take up half the book. The line of the story is broken again and again by these excursions into the past, and by switches from one plot to another, so that the coherence of the novel at times seems to hang by a thread in the midst of the spatial and temporal disunity Faulkner imposes upon it. It is fair to say that from this point of view the novel may leave something to be desired. However, the many adverse criticisms leveled at this lack of unity are not really justified: either they emanate from perfectionists who would wish this novel, whose beauties they duly admire, to be completely faultless, as they would demand that *Huckleberry Finn* have a perfect form, which is far from the case; or they come from critics who do not take into consideration the novelist's concept and purpose.

[*12*]

Any attempt to show the unity of *Light in August* by reducing its diverse themes to one only would be as futile as an effort to do justice to its much-debated structure through a panoramic view. Judgment should be based on methodical analysis, with the author's intentions borne well in mind throughout. It follows then, that one should study each chapter or group of chapters to see how and why the spatial and temporal breaks occur. Afterward, the results of the analysis should be coordinated and examined to define Faulkner's technique in the novel. Finally, some information, or rather speculation, about the novel's genesis may help toward an insight into its form.

THE STRUCTURE OF *LIGHT IN AUGUST*

CHAPTERS 1–4

Critics usually divide *Light in August* into three parts, the second comprising chapters 6–12, the huge flashback of Joe Christmas's life slotted into the action in the present, beginning just before Joanna Burden's murder and finishing shortly after it. But this division, based solely on chronological grounds, can only be superficial and does not help toward an understanding of the structure or of the author's overall design. It accords better with the text and with Faulkner's intentions if chapters 1–4 are seen as a first section: by the end of chapter 4 all the characters have been introduced and the main facts outlined; before plunging into the past, the novel completes a full circle back to its starting point with the picture of Lena arriving in Jefferson.

The first three chapters describe the arrival of each of the three main characters: Lena Grove in search of Lucas Burch, by whom she is pregnant (the start of the action in the present), Joe Christmas one Friday three years earlier (chapter 2), and the Reverend Hightower twenty-five years before (chapter 3). The histories of these three are not independent, like the alternating chapters of *The Wild Palms;* on the contrary, they are intertwined right from the start. The arrivals in Jefferson of Christmas, and then of Brown, are stored in Byron Bunch's memory. The description of Hightower's arrival and of his life in the town comes from the same source, although Byron has learned most of this from the people of Jefferson. In the second part of chapter 2, this same Byron Bunch falls in love with Lena Grove as soon as she comes into his workshop, and he discovers to his horror that Brown, now Christmas's associate in selling moonshine, is none other than Lucas Burch, Lena's seducer. Hightower, the former minister to whom Byron pays regular visits, is also introduced in this chapter (pp. 43–44).

During these first three chapters, Faulkner has managed to pass in review all the main characters, including Miss Burden, whose life history is sketched in chapter 2 (p. 42). As far as the action in the present is concerned, there are only the Hineses (the instruments and the visible signs of Christmas's past) and Percy Grimm (who is in a way outside time in his role as the instrument of fate) remaining to be introduced. Faulkner has linked the main characters together, making it clear that *Light in August* in not made up of three separate plots. In addition, the thematic structure of the book is already suggested: Lena, living in the present, trusting in nature, life, and love, partaking of the community of mankind, is the counterbalance to Christmas, locked in his sterile violence, an outcast from society and, in total contrast to Lena, nearly always described in the past tense. Even though there may be no concrete facts to support this concept of Christmas, Faulkner suggests it by making him a menacing and fatal figure: in the same way as for Chillingworth in *The Scarlet Letter,* the adjectives and images describing Christmas are indicative of his future role. Thus, as early as in the first two chapters, the two polar opposites of the novel are set side by side: this same contrast reappears within the structure of chapters 13 and 14, and again in the alternation of chapters 16, 17, 19, and 21.

Chapter 4 (the Sunday after the murder, when Byron tells Hightower the events of the previous day) reveals that Christmas is part Negro, according to Brown, that for three years he has been the lover of Miss Burden, whose throat he has cut, and that Brown is joining the manhunt in greedy pursuit of the thousand dollar reward. The main facts in the action are given in this chapter; the plots are brought to a climax, and already the reader can easily predict what will happen to each character: indeed, Faulkner suggests each one's fate in the last two pages. When Byron's account ends, Hightower expresses his anxiety: "Is it certain, proved, that he has negro blood? Think, Byron; what it will mean when the people—if they catch . . . Poor man. Poor mankind" (p. 93). Twice in an effort to procrastinate the horror he foresees, he says, or rather repeats to himself: "But they have not caught him yet. They have not caught him yet, Byron." But there is no doubt of the outcome of this manhunt in the South, where the fate of a Negro guilty of both murder and rape is as predictable as a ritual. Hightower begins to emerge from his hitherto impregnable ivory tower: the signs of rejection, retreat, and even of flight which punctuate the chapter disappear from his face, down which the sweat flows like tears (p. 93), presaging the real tears which will flow like sweat (p. 344) when he learns of Christmas's arrest. In the end we also know that, when Lena asks him to, Byron will do his duty and bring her face to face with the father of her child, in spite of his own love for her; but from what we already know of Brown, his betrayal of Christmas, and his animal pursuit of him alongside the police hounds, the ending can be foreseen. So the plot is in effect completed: or, more accurately, the "cops and robbers" plot is completed. So far Faulkner has only told us facts, and not their causes; as yet the novel has no meaning, any more than has its title; the characters have only been outwardly described, through rumor, the eye-witness accounts, narrations, and the summaries by the author; the reader knows little more than does the Jefferson public. For those who wish to understand what has happened and what is bound to happen, the novel really only begins after chapter 4, which closes the first part of the novel by bringing it back to its outset, and the picture of Lena getting down from the wagon, calm, her belly distended, and her words echoing what she said at the beginning of the book: "My, my. Here I have come clean from Alabama, and now I am in Jefferson at last, sure enough." Now these words are reported by Byron, which is impossible as he did not see Lena until she came to his workshop (p. 45), after her arrival in Jefferson. The author's artistic intention is therefore obvious: he wishes the first four chapters to form a perfect circle in themselves.

CHAPTER 5: ITS CONNECTIONS WITH CHAPTERS 6–12

Chapter 5 is a first flashback, into Christmas's immediate past, and it reconstructs his life in the last twenty-four hours before the murder. Chapters 6–12 go back to his earliest memories. Later, chapter 16 goes even further back, to his birth, his conception, and even to his grandparents' lifetime. Chronologically, chapter 5 should follow rather than precede chapters 6–12, or to be exact, it should come about five pages before the end of chapter 12, when the eve of the crime is again described. But a close reading of chapter 5, comparing it with the six which follow and the end of it with the corresponding passage at the end of chapter 12, proves that it is in its proper place, and for two reasons: first, because it touches on the same themes and images as are expanded and loaded with significance in the following chapters, and second, because it prepares the ground for the lengthy plunge into Christmas's past and explains its necessity.

It goes from midnight to midnight, and is the epitome of Christmas's life. It already makes use of the images which are always connected with him thereafter, images of darkness, filth, thick, foul water, the threatening abyss, the corridor or the street. The themes are a sort of model of those of chapters 6–12, as in these twenty–four hours, Christmas finally and totally rejects what he has always had to reject to try to preserve his own identity. He rejects the perverted Calvinism of McEachern and Miss Burden, as shown in his repeated protestation: "It's because she started praying over me." His repudiation of women and sexuality, to him synonymous with evil, is symbolized by his tearing off the last button from his underclothes, a sign of feminine work, and then his going to sleep in the stables, where he can breathe masculine odors. He rejects the white race, which has constantly tried to impose upon him an alien identity, and rages against it, facing the approaching car, whose headlights make his naked body gleam white in the surrounding darkness: "White bastards! . . . That's not the first of your bitches that ever saw . . ." (p. 100). Equally he rejects the black race, as he has all his life, fearing that it will at last engulf him: this is why, when he loses himself in Freedman Town, the black quarter, into which he has descended as into Hell, he flees in terror and then a moment later turns to rant at a group of Negroes he has just passed in the road: "Bitches! . . . Sons of bitches!" (p. 110). This chapter is thus the beginning of a search for understanding Christmas's life and death, his crime and his punishment.

It also prepares and introduces the long journey into Christmas's past. Faulkner intimates that chapters 6–12 are less a return to the past on the part of the reader than the return of the past to Christmas's mind. Even on the night before the murder, he was aware of the dormant, forgotten voices of the past: "it seemed to him . . . that he was hearing a myriad sounds . . . voices, murmurs, whispers: of trees, darkness, earth; people: his own voice; other voices evocative of names and times and places—which he had been conscious of all his life without knowing it, which were his life . . ." (pp. 97–98). These same voices are recalled shortly before the crime, in Chapter 12: "The dark was filled with the voices, myriad, out of all time that he had known, as though all the past was a flat pattern" (p. 266). Just before the end of chapter 5 and the resurgence of those images to Christmas's mind, Faulkner deliberately states that the voices had not begun again. When Christmas thinks: *"Something is going to happen to me"* (and this is the last sentence of the chapter), it is likely that he senses this approaching eruption of his past rather than his crime. In fact, before it is ever committed, the crime is already a part of the past, and Christmas thinks of it as an accomplished deed: "He was saying to himself *I had to do it* already in the past tense; *I had to do it. She said so herself*" (p. 264). He knows dimly that his body is going to act without any prompting from him—because he feels that the act is already completed—and that it is the inevitable consummation of the sum of the experiences he feels rising again within him. His present and his future are contained in his past, *are* in fact his past since it has become his present once more through his own consciousness of it—an idea to which Faulkner gives faintly Shakespearean expression: "And going on: tomorrow night, all the tomorrows, to be a part of the flat pattern, going on . . . since tomorrow to-be and had-been would be the same" (p. 266). However, the story of his life, as we shall see, is compounded less of his memories than of the author's development of what is latent in the character.[1]

Another skilful technicality points to the particular nature of chapters 6–12: the murder is never actually described. At the end of chapter 5, Christmas gets up and sets off for Joanna's house. Here the narration is sharply broken off because his thoughts and his acts are no longer connected, and memories of the past, from childhood and adolescence right up to the minutes before the murder, float to the surface of his mind. Again, toward the end of chapter 12, his thoughts break away from his actions, and again the murder is not described. The last pages of the chapter adroitly show the end of the dislocation, as mind and body once more work together. Joe finds himself in the middle of the road and stops a car, which gives him a ride, but for some reason he does not understand, its occupants are terrified of him. Later, he stumbles as the car speeds away from him and he feels something hard and heavy knock against his leg: "The object which had struck him had delivered an appreciable blow; then he discovered that the object was attached to his right hand. Raising the hand, he found that *it* held the ancient heavy pistol. *He* did not know that he had it; he did not remember having picked it up at all, nor why" (p. 270; my italics). He sees his hand holding the pistol and only then realizes that *he* is holding it; the transition from *it* to *he* marks the return to conscious reality, and leads subsequently to understanding of the whole incident.

Christmas's dislocation is the less surprising as Faulkner has prepared for it in chapter 5. Joe is not in a normal state of mind; he is in a traumatic condition as a result of his life with Joanna, who has gone from an extreme of sexual perversion to an extreme of religious fanaticism; he is afraid both of being forced by her to pray and of the dark abyss she represents for him: thus he is terrified when he feels trapped in the depths of Freedman Town, a dark, feminine abyss. As the day goes by, he gradually loses all sense of time and it seems to him that he is suspended outside himself, above his life and its successive actions: "hanging motionless and without physical weight he seemed to watch the slow flowing of time beneath him . . ." (p. 104). In the evening, from seven o'clock onward, mechanical, fatal time once more punctuates his life, until he sets off toward Miss Burden's house: through this technique, Faulkner emphasizes the disparity between the external reality and the images and voices filling Christmas's mind. These last are arranged and amplified in chapters 6–12.

CHAPTERS 6–12

It soon becomes difficult to tell whether these chapters are Christmas's thoughts or an intervention from the omniscient author. The freedom allowed by Faulkner's subtle technique makes distinction well-nigh impossible. Chapter 6 opens with some indication as to the nature of the narrative: "Memory believes before knowing remembers," and this is again referred to at the beginning of chapters 7 and 10. However, within this framework the author has total liberty to recall from his subject's past everything about him, whether latent, subconscious, forgotten, or even unknown to him—anything which contributes to an understanding of him.

Chapter 6 is devoted to Joe's life at the orphanage until he was taken by Mr. and Mrs. McEachern. Right from his earliest years and the incident of the dietitian and the toothpaste, femininity and evil have the same smell and taste, and are irremediably synonymous in his mind.

Chapter 7 is a detailed extension of chapter 6. Joe's life until he is sixteen is given through symptomatic episodes, each of which shows his animosity toward femininity, that is, evil. When he is eight, Joe persists for a whole day in refusing to learn his catechism and ecstatically takes his punishment, still rejecting McEachern's uncompromising religion. The episode is given its complete significance in the diptych to this passage, where Joe stolidly and scornfully refuses Mrs. McEachern's pity, rejecting the food she brings him secretly. Only when she has gone does he fall like a dog on the food he threw on the floor while she was there. At fourteen, he finds himself with a group of boys eager to lose their virginity. When he goes into the shed where the Negro girl awaits him he hovers on the edge of the same abyss which menaces him later with Joanna. He attacks the woman and suffers a beating from the other boys, a behavior pattern which soon becomes characteristic of him. Then when he is eighteen, he sells his heifer in order to buy a suit, and Mr. McEachern discovers this. Mrs. McEachern tries to shield the boy by saying she bought the suit and Mr. McEachern forces her to beg pardon on her knees. This incident completes and summarizes the other two. Joe rejects McEachern and the pitiless religion which forces an eighteen-year-old boy and an old woman to their knees: it is Joanna's demand for the same abasement which he later sees as the main motive for his crime. For the first time he actively resists his foster father's blows. He equally rebuffs Mrs. McEachern's overwhelming femininity, which always gives him the same sense of guilt: when he looks back on his relationship with his foster mother, he is confirmed in his opinion that women have such an affinity for evil that it gives everything they touch an "odor," an "aftertaste" (p. 157).

Joe's affair with the waitress Bobbie Allen is described in chapter 8, which starts only a few hours after the last incident, as Joe goes to put on the controversial suit before leaving to meet Bobbie. The story then goes back to tell of the first time Joe saw her, a year before. So, chronologically, this chapter, except for the first two pages, fits inside chapter 7. However, Faulkner has clearly arranged the account of Joe's life to give each chapter the greatest possible unity in its matter as well as in its meaning. This chapter is concerned with Joe's sexual experiences, which are inseparable from his knowledge of evil (a connection borne out by his discovery that Bobbie is a prostitute), and inseparable too from the physical repulsion dating from the discovery of the true nature of Bobbie's "indisposition" at their first rendezvous: this revelation sent him off to vomit among the tree trunks, symbols of virility. These first experiences indicate some of Christmas's obsessions, to which Faulkner makes no further reference until Joe meets Joanna when he is thirty–three. The chapter finishes with a mention of the heifer, so bringing it back to its point of departure.

The beginning of chapter 9 goes back to the opening of chapter 8, as Joe slides past McEachern's window on his rope. Immediately guessing that Joe's only motive for this nighttime escape must be lechery, McEachern follows and finds him as inevitably as if he were guided by St. Michael himself and personally charged with the chastising of the Devil. Joe knocks him down, and flees in pursuit of Bobbie, shouting, exactly as after the murder of Joanna, "I have done it! I have done it!" (p. 194; cf. p. 88). On his arrival at Max's he is like an automaton and unaware of what passes around him: his thoughts and actions are as disconnected as when he has killed Joanna. Then he antagonizes the two men, is beaten by them and left half-conscious in the empty house.

Chapter 10 whisks Joe from Bobbie to Joanna in a powerful panorama of his life until he is thirty-three: these years are spanned by the image of the street he enters on leaving Max's house and which holds him captive, offering neither safety nor peace, until it leads him to Miss Burden's kitchen. Chapters 11 and 12 show the three phases in the relationship between Joe and Joanna. The first phase goes from his brutal rape of her to the day when she comes to his cabin to talk to him about her family. Her account is interesting in that it shows analogies between her ancestors and those of Joe and Hightower, and suggests that her Calvinism is of the same brand as that of the other fanatics in the book. However, it is too long, breaking into the main story as it does, and distracting the reader with some irrelevant detail. Indeed, Faulkner does sometimes refuse to sacrifice his pleasure in telling a story to the demands of a narrative, although he is far more restrained in this than that other compulsive storyteller, Mark Twain.

The last two phases of their relationship take up chapter 12. First, it is to Joe as though he has fallen into a sewer, and he is filled with terror at the sight of the abyss. With the approach of Joanna's menopause the relationship dies. Then in the third phase, cold and masculine again, Joanna suggests that Joe should go to a Negro school and then become her business manager. Faced with his indignant refusal, Joanna, damned and despairing as she is, can but ask him to kneel down with her and pray. She even suggests that their only solution is that they should both die. The chapter ends after the murder, when Joe hurls her pistol into the bushes.

CHAPTER 13

After successfully following and intertwining the three plots during the first four chapters, Faulkner has now disturbed this balance and abandoned Lena and Hightower for seven chapters to concentrate on Joe. With chapter 13 he picks up the threads of the beginning once more.

Chapter 13 has two sections. The first is an objective, external description of the reactions of the Jefferson public to the discovery of the fire and the murder on Saturday morning; it goes on until Monday's dawn, when we see the men and dogs waiting for daylight to find their way out of the woods. There are no new facts, but those related by Byron on the Sunday evening (chapter 4) are rearranged and embroidered. Now, however, the tone is lighter and a little more ironic, as though Faulkner wished to put Joe's story back into perspective with the other two plots, and also to give added poignancy, by contrast with the second half of the chapter, to the tragedies of Joe and Hightower, of which the public knows nothing: as far as Jefferson is concerned, Hightower's story ended twenty-five years before and that Joe's will end very soon is a foregone conclusion.

The second part of the chapter is marked by a return to the present tense (p. 282), which, apart from very briefly in chapters 6, 7, and 10, has not been used since chapter 4. Twice Byron visits Hightower and, again facing him across his desk, continues his exposition of events, only interrupted by the questions and remarks of his listener. On the first evening he talks of his plans and concern for Lena. The following evening, Wednesday, he is completely changed, sure of himself; he has settled Lena into Brown's old cabin so that she is under a roof of her own to await the birth of her child. Between these two evenings there is a scene (pp. 291–94) in which Hightower learns that Christmas's tracks have been picked up again and refuses to jeopardize his sanctuary of peace by taking action: " 'I wont! I wont! I have bought immunity. I have paid' " (p. 292). The two worlds set as polar opposites in the first chapters of *Light in August,* that of violence, death, and alienation contrasting with the world of trust in nature and love, are again in violent juxtapositon, but the confrontation now takes place in Hightower's mind, which is hereafter the central consciousness of the novel. From now on, the main theme of the novel is Hightower's painful transition from one world to the other, until finally, following Christmas, he suffers his passion and sees the light of August. However, at the end of this chapter, Hightower is still so far from accepting sacrifice, in himself or others, that he advises Byron to leave Lena: and then he turns to his Tennyson, the symbol of his rejection of life and fertility, which he has kept by him ever since he left the seminary (p. 301). Nevertheless, his sanctuary is beginning to crumble about him, as is suggested in an image already pointing to that of the wheel which heralds his completed "revolution" and return to life: "it was . . . like the earth itself were rocking faintly, preparing to move. Then it seemed to move, like something released slowly and without haste, in an augmenting swoop . . ." (p. 292). Timidly, he offers to help Byron and thinks when he has gone: "'God bless him' . . . . *To be young. There is nothing else like it: there is nothing else in the world*" (p. 300).

CHAPTERS 14 AND 15

Chapter 14 continues with this confrontation between the two worlds of the novel. After a brief look, in the present tense, at Lena's life and at her calm confidence, Faulkner returns to Christmas, describing the time between the murder and his arrest. At the beginning of these seven days, an ironic inversion of Holy Week, Christmas still inhabits his world of violence and death. Later, however, it seems as though he finds some sort of peace, a change which Faulkner emphasizes by describing him for the first time in Lena's tense, the present. By Wednesday, as the sound and the fury of the manhunt die away, one isolated phrase in the present tense is used to refer to him (p. 313). Then it is used again at dawn on Friday, when, peaceful or else weak from lack of food and a seven-day flight (it is difficult to tell which), Christmas renounces violence and perhaps comes close to Lena in the instant when he accepts death: "'I have been further in these seven days than in all the thirty years'" (p. 321). When he is released from the urgency he has felt within himself all week, or rather for more than thirty years, it is significant that he makes an effort to rediscover the earth, Lena's element, just as Hightower finds it later: "It is as though he desires to see his native earth in all its phases for the first or the last time" (p. 320). Although Hightower does not appear in this chapter, the course he will run is prefigured in Christmas's, even though Joe's last days may allow of a different interpretation.[2]

Chapter 15 confirms Joe's apparent transformation, although it is still uncertain whether it means acceptance or resignation. Among the hostile crowd, Halliday, who strikes him twice on the face, and Doc Hines, whose demented oratory incites the people to a lynching, he stands out as the only calm person. Bleeding and silent, he submits to the blows unresistingly. But this chapter really revolves around Doc Hines, and Christmas is seen in the distance, through the reactions of the crowd and of Hines and his wife. Hines's violence is perceived in its full force only in retrospect in the next chapter when we learn that he is Joe's grandfather: the revelation makes his incitement to lynching even more horrific. Once more Faulkner has perhaps allowed himself to be carried away by his characters: a number of the details about Hines seem here useless and merely distracting. In fact, Hines's character is even more remarkable in the following chapter, where his own words fully reveal the fanatical violence which his wife rightly describes as demoniac rather than religious.

CHAPTERS 16–18

Through the incoherent ramblings of the love-starved Mrs. Hines and of Doc Hines, who sees himself as God's chosen instrument on earth, chapter 16 goes yet further into Joe's life and antecedents than did chapter 6. There, the description of his conscious and subconscious life explained how he came to kill his foster father (if he did) and Joanna: but now that Joe has resigned himself to his fatality, Faulkner has to concretize the chain of destiny which has imprisoned him throughout his life. This chapter undertakes this task, and in spite of its chronological displacement, its insertion at this point is fully justifiable.

The scene in which Hines preaches in a Negro church and threatens the Negroes with extermination by the whites gives an aura of destiny to Joe's own murderous violence in another black church. The violence which has been part of Joe from his birth now seems to be hereditary, driving him to repeat actions of which he knows nothing. Now

that his violent death is only days or hours away, the account
of his birth and early years is invested with a greater sense
of tragedy than it would have had two hundred pages
earlier. Faulkner was to use the same technique in *The
Hamlet* to describe the life and death of Jack Houston,
as he had in *Sanctuary* to tell of Popeye's childhood, just
before the latter's execution. Moreover, the details of Joe's
life in the orphanage are not in any way a repetition of
chapter 6. Then Faulkner showed how women and evil
had become synonymous in the child's mind; now Hines's
insane monologue (pp. 361–65) is mostly about Joe's Negro
blood, with which the small children unwittingly reproached
him; he himself showed an early and peculiar interest in
the subject, questioning Doc Hines and the Negro who
worked in the yard. These details have a special importance
at this juncture: for the first time Joe has come to think
of Negroes as his brothers (p. 317), and he has symbolically
appropriated a pair of Negro brogans, "that mark on his
ankles the gauge definite and ineradicable of the black
tide creeping up his legs, moving from his feet upward
as death moves" (p. 321). Finally, the account of Joe's birth
into an atmosphere of hate and violence, placed where
it is in the novel, gives added symbolic meaning to the
birth of Lena's son, who comes to represent the return
of life and love to a sterile world. The parallel between
the two births, reinforced by the confusion of Mrs. Hines,
who thinks Lena is her daughter Milly, dead in childbirth,
and the infant her own grandson so soon snatched from
her, underlines the contrast between the two worlds, or
the two poles on which the novel turns. Thus, the position
of chapters 16 and 17 is completely justified: had they
been placed simply in their chronological order, the structure
of *Light in August* would have been less coherent.

Chapters 16 and 17 are also used to advance the
movement initiated in chapter 13: Hightower's painful
progress continues away from the negative values repre-

sented by Joe and Joanna and toward the positive ones of Lena and Byron. Shortly after the beginning of chapter 16, Faulkner skillfully prepares for the despairing and demented monologues of Doc Hines and his wife in Hightower's presence. The organ music tells in essence the story of Joe's origins and life. It suggests the repudiation of life and of love, the fascination of violence and death, the need to crucify oneself and other people, "pleading, asking, for not love, not life, forbidding it to others, demanding in sonorous tones death as though death were the boon, like all Protestant music" (p. 347): it is an overture to the meeting with the Hines couple. Hightower understands both messages, yet refuses to accept either. By the end of the chapter, he feels like a defendant in court ("The other three sit facing him; almost like a jury," p. 365), when Byron, fully aware of the irony of the situation, puts his back to the wall by asking him to save Joe. At this point, Byron can readily identify Hightower's real enemy: *"It aint me he is shouting at. It's like he knows there is something nearer him than me to convince of that"* (p. 370). Thus, in plunging more deeply into Christmas's past and origins, chapter 16 prefigures chapter 20, where Hightower must consciously make a similar journey into his past, to the time before he came to Jefferson, even to his ancestors. However, the contact with Joe's grandparents is not alone sufficient to cause this: only the brutal shock of a meeting with Christmas himself can finally provoke it. Before then, Hightower, the passive, seated man, has to get up and act. This is the subject of chapter 17, which leads on from the final image of chapter 16, where Hightower is seen with his fists still clenched, but "lying full in the pool of light from the shaded lamp."

Hightower delivers Lena's baby before the doctor even arrives, and by the same token effects his own rebirth (the baby he delivered to a Negro woman a few years previously was stillborn): "there goes through him a glow, a wave, a surge of something almost hot, almost triumphant. 'I showed them!' he thinks. 'Life comes to the old man yet, while they get there too late' " (pp. 382-83). He feels twenty-five again, and substitutes *Henry IV*, "food for a man," for Tennyson (p. 383). Like Christmas shortly before his death, Hightower is aware of "the savage and fecund odor of the earth" (p. 384), to which Lena and her kind belong.

This childbirth is a crucial event for Hightower. It is equally so for Byron, who is finally forced to accept what he has so far unconsciously refused to acknowledge: that the woman he loves is not a virgin. Yet since Byron is already converted to the values Lena represents, his experience is less significant than Hightower's. In fact, the passages relating to Byron in chapters 17 and 18 are perhaps a little overweighted. However, the sudden importance given to Brown in chapter 18 seems to be more of a flaw. His journey to Lena's cabin with the deputy who appears to promise him his thousand dollar reward may be amusing, but it tells us nothing new about Brown. Moreover, his minutely drawn impotent fury is here described as "ecstatic" (p. 411), and the use of this term, hitherto applied only to Christmas, confers an incongruous tragic stature on this character who is usually likened to an animal or an empty automobile. Perhaps though, it is less a case of incoherence on Faulkner's part then of fidelity to characters who, like the six characters of Pirandello, are so real to him that they sometimes escape and lead their own lives.

CHAPTER 19

Although Christmas's death is already known at the end of chapter 18, the knowledge does not detract from the interest of chapter 19. The explanation of an event is always more important to Faulkner than the event itself: and yet this chapter is ironic in that it shows the ultimate futility of all explanations and, finally, leaves the reader with nothing but facts which retain all their mystery. In the first part, the intellectual, the Harvard alumnus, Gavin Stevens, seeks to give a rational account of Joe's conduct. Yet, in spite of its brilliance, his theory of the alternating influence of white and Negro blood sheds no light on Christmas's last moments and is meangingless in the face of his tragedy. It strikes the reader as an arbitrary explanation, especially in the end. What is more, it is ironic that Gavin confidently assumes that Christmas is actually of mixed race, although Faulkner's consummate artistry has always left this doubtful. In a way, Gavin's attempt to rationalize is a warning with respect to the whole book, a reminder that no rational explanations can reach the core of the mystery of any man's life.

It is in the story of Percy Grimm and his pursuit of Christmas, in the second part of the chapter, that we find a valid commentary on that death. Grimm is inspired with the same conviction which drove McEachern and Doc Hines, and at first his implacable pursuit seems to be a repetition of theirs. The difference is that Grimm has more in common with his quarry than either of the others: they are both pawns on a board, moved by a "Player." This likeness is confirmed in the following chapter, when Hightower seems to see their faces blended together indistinguishably. So any attempt at explanation eventually founders on what is either inexplicable or ineluctable, and Faulkner keeps to the facts of Christmas's death and castration. Even though the symbolic atmosphere of the last lines may furnish a neat conclusion to the chapter and a meaning for Christmas's death, it leaves the tragedy of his life inviolate.

However, the question arises here of whether Faulkner wished to suggest a convergence of the paths of the two characters who were at the beginning diametrically opposed, Lena and Christmas. In doing so, he would weave the threads of his story together even more firmly. The word "serene," persistently applied to Lena, is used here of Joe for the first time (in the days immediately before his death he was only calm, peaceful): Christmas's serenity in death could be a parallel in the tragic mood to Lena's comic serenity in life and in the pains of childbirth. As has previously been noted with reference to chapter 14, during his "Holy Week" Christmas discovered the earth, intrinsically Lena's element (p. 320). Finally, as he waits at the roadside for the passing wagons and then, seated in one, is lulled by its movement into the loss of all sense of time, going calmly to give himself up in Mottstown, Joe infallibly reminds us of Lena as we saw her at the beginning of the novel, still and serene in her wanderings, as though eternally suspended in the August light.

CHAPTER 20

Chapter 20 brings Hightower to the end of his journey, to his passion and redemption. He at last admits his crime. He has used the Church and his parishioners as a means to get him to Jefferson, where he could, as he sat at his window each evening in the fading light, recapture the gallant vision of his grandfather, who had died returning from a cavalry raid, indeed remarkable for its boyish irresponsibility and overwhelming contempt for life. Worse, he has used his wife as a means to the same end, never seeing her as a being in her own right and one whose suffering and yearning should have given her a greater claim on his compassion than his parishioners. He acknowledges that his wasted life, his twenty-five years of suffering and persecution, have represented for him not an expiation but a voluptuous martyrdom. He saw it as the price he had to pay for his grandfather's ghost, for his own immunity, for the right to cut himself off from humanity and even to destroy himself. Now he understands that one cannot buy immunity, since each man's responsibility goes beyond himself to the whole of mankind, of which he is a part. For the first time he really admits the existence of someone beyond himself, hence of all humanity: "if I am the instrument of her despair and death, then I am in turn instrument of someone outside myself" (p. 465).

Before Hightower could emerge from his deathlike egoism, and reenter humanity, many things had to happen. Christmas had to indicate the path to be followed through his own renunciation of a violent past and his return to the brotherhood of mankind, whether or not he relented through lassitude or true resignation (chapter 14). Then, knowing that Joe had been born into a loveless world (chapter 16), Hightower had to bring back life and love by delivering Lena's baby (chapter 17). Finally, in the path of Christmas, who suffered and died, and who saw perhaps in his last peaceful and unbearable look Lena's earth (chapter 19), Hightower too must suffer and die to his sterile past (chapter 20). Admitting that chapters 15 (the Hineses' story and their doings on the day of Joe's arrest) and 18 (Byron with Mrs. Beard and with the sheriff, and Brown's flight) may give more substance to the characters yet add little to the novel, the order of the narrative from chapter 14 onward is completely justifiable, once chapter 13 has intertwined the plots again and shown the direction the book will take. In fact, it is only through this order that the meaning of *Light in August* becomes clear.

Chapter 20 closes with the vision Hightower awaits each evening in the delicately suspended twilight—the vision of his grandfather with his cavalry squadron in their heroic and absurd charge. This paragraph and its position could throw doubt on the interpretation of Hightower propounded in this study. For instance, Richard Chase[3] sees Hightower's deathlike immobility as a sign that he has chosen madness, or even death,[4] which completes the circle of his destiny as represented in the image of the wheel. Faulkner does not seem to find this passage ambiguous:

> He didn't die. He had wrecked his life. He had failed his wife. He had failed himself, but there was one thing that

he still had—which was the brave grandfather that galloped into the town to burn the Yankee stores, and at least he had that. . . . He had to endure, to live, but that was one thing that was pure and fine that he had—was the memory of his grandfather, who had been brave.[5]

So it appears that Hightower carried on living with a vision that was no longer sterile, but an image of courage, in the spirit of *Henry IV*, not of Tennyson. As Richard P. Adams says, "he falls back on his vision of the past. But it is a dynamic vision, and perhaps now he is able to see it less as a retreat from life and more as an encouragement to help him endure whatever life remains with a better grace than he has had before."[6] His vision has at last become liberating rather than imprisoning. It is surely significant that it has never been described before. In chapter 3 we see Hightower just before he has his vision (p. 55) and then when it is over: at this point, Faulkner mentions the "August darkness" (p. 70), as though the light could not come until the vision had been arduously earned. There is a further possible interpretation of this passage: this vision, described here for the first time, could be the last—no longer the possession of the present by the ghosts of the past, but the cathartic liberation from this past. Hightower would then retain nothing other than the *memory* of this past—an interpretation that seems to be confirmed by Faulkner's own commentary on his text. Whatever the interpretation, Hightower does remain an ambiguous figure. But as we shall see, this is equally true of Joe and Lena.

CHAPTER 21

At first sight, the last chapter is an epilogue which adds nothing new, as one supposes that Byron will marry Lena. This was clearly suggested in chapter 18, when Lena cried at the thought that she might not see Byron again. Hightower had already visualized the outcome: *"That will* be her life, her destiny. *The good stock peopling in tranquil obedience to it the good earth; from these hearty loins without hurry or haste descending mother and daughter. But by Byron engendered next"* (p. 384). However, the chapter is still important, since it serves to return the reader to the beginning of the book. In the first chapter Lena was partly described through the eyes of Armstid, whose stolid farmer's common sense faced eternal womanhood. The furniture dealer of this last chapter is in a sense an avatar of Armstid, drawn in comical, almost licentious vein. Moreover, Lena's last words echo her first thought. The frieze on the Geeek vase evoked in the first chapter again passes without motion before the reader's eyes, while the urn revolves back to its original position. Thus *Light in August* describes a full circle and achieves a unity of form which seemed unlikely to survive after the first four chapters, given the problems posed in coordinating three centers of interest.

Yet the importance of this chapter is more than structural. The comic situation of Lena and Byron, who are not yet a couple, is described with great zest by the furniture dealer as he lies in bed with his wife after a week's absence. This conversation between husband and wife, happy, warm, humorous, and in which Faulkner is sentimental in the best sense of the word, at last shows the relationship of a normal couple, lifts the novel out of tragedy, and calmly affirms the continuity of human nature, its endurance, to use a truly Faulknerian term. The end of *Light in August* is thus dominated by the image of the procreating couple (whether married or not matters little, since Nature takes no notice of the conventions): the solidity of the relationship between the anonymous furniture dealer and his wife is, one might say, an insurance on the life that Lena and Byron will lead. In fact, these two are also anonymous, the one, like the nameless woman in the "Old Man" section of *The Wild Palms,* a symbol of fertility and continuity (hence the significance of the journey resumed after childbirth), the other so insignificant that one would never see him "'the first glance if he was alone by himself in the bottom of a empty concrete swimming pool'" (p. 469), as the furniture dealer so vividly explains to his wife. And the novel closes with the picture of Lena, now suckling an apparently insatiable baby, "that hadn't never stopped eating, that had been eating breakfast now for about ten miles . . ." (p. 480). Thus the ending fully justifies the title *Light in August* and clearly illuminates the significance of the whole novel, which seems to mark a stage, perhaps a victory, in the career of its author: *Sanctuary,* published eighteen months earlier, ended in the Luxembourg Gardens in the dying light of a dusk already autumnal although it was still summer; far from opening it up to life, Faulkner closed that novel with evocations of rain and death.

The length of this analysis is due to the fact that it could not have been done without precise references to the themes and characters, as the meaning of the novel necessarily springs from the structure. In the course of the study, several traits of Faulkner's technique have been outlined; it now remains to look at them more closely.

FAULKNER'S TECHNIQUE IN *LIGHT IN AUGUST*

LINKS BETWEEN THE PLOTS

To describe *Light in August* as a "triad of actions," as Irving Howe has done, does not take into account Faulkner's technique. There are many links of various sorts joining the three centers of interest so that there cannot be any doubt as to their interdependence and the unity of the novel. Malcolm Cowley became aware of this when he vainly tried to extract Joe's story to include it in *The Portable Faulkner.* He wrote to the author: "The anthologist can't pick him out without leaving bits of his flesh hanging to Hightower and Lena."[7] He had to make do with the story of Percy Grimm instead.

It has already been noted that, even in the first three chapters, Faulkner links the fates of the characters. Toward the end of the book their paths cross one another physically. Having been told the stories of both Lena and Joe, Hightower then comes face to face with Lena, Joe's grandparents, and finally, with Joe himself, at the climax of the novel. Lena takes up residence in the cabin previously used by Joe and Brown, and there under the gaze of Joe's grandmother, has a son, whom the old lady confuses with Joe himself. The confusion even affects Lena: "I am afraid she might get me mixed up, like they say how you might cross your eyes and then you can't uncross . . ." (p. 388; Faulkner's ellipsis). Thus the characters are connected in a physical sense, and also, more importantly, in a symbolic sense: Joe is, in a way, reborn in Lena's son, who has given new life to Hightower, simultaneously deliverer and delivered. The conclusion of the novel is a statement of faith in the victory of life over death, of fertility over sterility: that is the meaning of the last chapter.

THE ROLE OF BYRON

The physical coordination of the characters is effected by Byron, who occupies a central position in the novel, as the only person in touch with all the others, and so is capable of bringing them together. When the novel opens he has worked with Christmas and is Hightower's confidant. However, he is not locked in a past of death and violence, nor is he cut off from the community, since, although he lives alone, he leads the choir in a country church every week. He can, and does, fall in love with Lena at first sight and devote himself to her in spite of Hightower's disapproval, yet he continues his friendship with the former minister. This puts Byron into the position of a mediator, and makes him at once witness, narrator, and actor, which is exactly what Faulkner needs to knit the threads of the novel together. At the beginning he is largely a witness:

he remembers the arrivals of Christmas and of Brown in chapter 2 ("Byron Bunch knows this") and Hightower's life story in chapter 3. Then he becomes a narrator and gives Hightower indirect contact with Christmas and Lena (chapters 4 and 13). Finally Byron disappears as a narrator, and he is thereafter directly or indirectly responsible for bringing the different characters together: Brown and Lena, Lena and Hightower, the Hineses and Hightower, Christmas and Hightower. It is thus thanks to him that Hightower moves from one world to the other, so resolving the plots.

Byron's double function of actor and narrator is largely responsible for the suspense of the novel. Even as he brings information, the narrator can indeed be a screen between the facts and the reader, inasmuch as the informant's emotions are a filter affecting the coherence of the account. Also, any narration presupposes that the narrator has learned the facts before he can recount them: hence there is a possibility that he may omit some details, indispensable to the reader, though not to him since he knows them. The beginning of chapter 4 is a case in point. Here Byron is obsessed with two memories which fill his mind to the exclusion of all else and which cause him to disregard the coherence of his story. The first is the memory of Lena sitting in the sawmill yard and guessing Brown's identity too soon. The second is that of Lena and himself in the square in Jefferson and then at Mrs. Beard's (this scene is so clearly imprinted on Byron's mind that Faulkner, for the only time in the chapter, goes from narration to a direct exposition of the facts through a classic cinematographic sequence; pp. 77–80): Byron was then so intent on keeping Lena in ignorance of Joanna's murder that in his narrative he leaves Hightower in the same ignorance. Moreover, as he is telling on Sunday evening what happened the day before, he neglects certain facts which he has only learned in the interim, while still alluding to them since he himself knows them. This explains Hightower's incomprehension ("But I don't see any connection between—" p. 72) and also Byron's ominous remarks, such as: "I didn't know myself, then, the other. The rest of it. The worst of it" (p. 75). In this way Faulkner arouses the reader's curiosity by making him share the uneasiness of a character in the same uncomprehending position as himself. The skill lies in his avoiding imposing suspense artificially, preferring to make full use of the opportunities offered by a narrator: his presence alone, suggesting a time lapse, and his state of mind, make the suspense natural.

RECURRING SCENES

So far the links discovered between the plots have been mainly factual, but even tighter bonds are created by motifs recurring within one plot or between plots, which thus acquire significance beyond the facts themselves. For instance, the repetition of certain types of scene, the consistent importance of certain places and objects, the many parallels inherent in the characters, all contribute to the close texture of the novel.

An instance of the way certain scenes relate to each other is found in connection with money. When Mrs. Armstid breaks open her china bank to give her egg money to Lena (pp. 18–19), she hides her true generosity and embarrassment under harsh abruptness. She understands Lena, and Lena understands her and accepts the gesture in its true spirit. On the other hand, the dietitian's attempt to buy Joe's silence with a silver dollar (p. 116) or Mrs. McEachern's minute additions to the slender hoard behind a loose board in Joe's room are both furtive moves; each attempt to win over the child makes him feel guilty, an accomplice of the evil he associates with women. The contrasts betweeen the respective attitudes of Joe and Lena, and of other people toward them, are underlined in these scenes.

The violence in the novel usually involves blows to the

face. Joe, like Christ, is struck in the face and remains alone and uncomplaining in the midst of a hostile crowd. At several other times during his life he has received facial blows, from McEachern, Bobbie Allen, and the men at Max's restaurant. He himself lashed out at every opportunity, methodically slugging Brown on two occasions, hitting Bobbie, slapping Brother Bedenberry in the Negro church, knocking down Roz Thompson and McEachern, bloodying Hightower's face, striking and wounding Joanna and finally cutting off her head. When it is revealed that Hines also fought and struck his wife, his daughter, and Joe, this characteristic violence comes to seem hereditary and Joe's actions part of an inescapable fatality.

As these examples suggest, recurring scenes are particularly important in Joe's life. Thus in three parallel pursuits the fanatic and impersonal pursuer in each case infallibly finds his victim as though guided by some superior power, or moved by the "Player" on the board. Doc Hines chases and kills Joe's father; McEachern, self-constituted avenging angel, finds Joe at the dance and strikes him; and Percy Grimm, angelic and satanic, kills and castrates him. The other pursuits all resemble these three, particularly the one in chapter 6. Here the dietitian, indirectly pursuing Joe, is led in spite of herself to Doc Hines, who is himself pursuing the child with his vigilant hate and who goes to see Miss Atkins to settle the details of Joe's abduction; he finds her room straightaway and forces himself inside, designating her Jezebel, as McEachern later calls Bobbie when he finds her dancing with Joe. Joanna, nymphomaniac then religious fanatic, also dogs Joe with a passion very near to hate. In fact, the motif of pursuit exemplifies Joe's whole life, which is one ceaseless headlong flight in an endless street, away from the dark abyss which menaces him, and finally catches up with him as he enters Mottstown to be arrested. Ironically, when Joe unerringly finds McEachern's horse, he seems to be endowed "with something of his adopted father's complete faith in an infallibility in events" (p. 194). It is even more ironic that Lena, the antithesis of Joe, tracks down her seducer with the same certainty as the other pursuers.

These are only a few examples of the many interlocking scenes which have the effect of subordinating the particular scene to the pattern it and its fellows create. Event becomes motif, and even myth, as William Empson remarks: "A situation is repeated for quite different characters, and this puts the main interest in the situation not the characters. . . . The situation is made something valuable in itself, perhaps for reasons hardly realized; it can work on you like a myth."[8]

FOCAL POINTS

Certain places act as focal points within the novel, helping to define it around fixed centers. Such is the case of the Burden house, which is, in a way the hub of the action (Faulkner was at first going to call this novel *Dark House*). The black women who go there have in fact worn converging paths, "which radiated from the house like wheelspokes" (p. 243); and at the beginning of the novel, this axis extends into space in the form of a column of yellow smoke seen by most of the characters. At this point, the house is the home of sterility and death. Yet it is here that Byron guides Lena, who so effectively restores it to life and fertility that even Hightower begins to live again in this place and responds once more to the secret rhythm of the earth. It is from here also that Brown resumes his onward flight, turning his back on Lena, life, and his responsibilities. Finally, Byron returns here having won the right to stay with Lena through the blows inflicted on him by Brown.

One scenic detail associated with several characters serves to link them together: the window. Hightower is above all the man at the window, through which he communicates with the past and is held prisoner by his ghosts; moreover, his wife, whom he had refused to love by remaining locked in his dead past, throws herself through the window of a Memphis hotel. Lena escapes through a window to go in search of Lucas Burch, whose child she bears, and Burch himself flees through a window, leaving her with the child. Lastly, Joe leaves by the window when he goes to meet Bobbie, the prostitute. Later he climbs through the kitchen window of Joanna, who prostitutes herself for him. Each of these two acts involves him in murderous assault. The window thus becomes the symbol "which connects and gathers around itself a series of meanings, sometimes conflicting, sometimes complementary, and by the recurrent use of which the novelist is able to merge together numerous elements of the book which, from the point of view of the plot alone, might otherwise seem disparate to the reader."⁹

The spatial unity of the novel is finally assured by the fact that nearly all the action in the present and a large part of the action in the past takes place in Jefferson. The townspeople are often heard; numerous background figures judge and comment on the events filling the foreground, and rumor, that anonymous voice, tells of Hightower's life since he arrived in Jefferson, in chapter 3 ("they told Byron . . ."). In this town both Joanna and Hightower have clearly defined positions in relation to the community; even if they are spiritually rejected, they remain two monuments making up part of the scenery: "the town realised at last that [Hightower] would be a part of its life until he died, and that they might as well become reconciled" (p. 67). The town, and especially its community, which is the chorus of the drama, thus form the backdrop against which Lena and Joe are counterpoised: in Jefferson they come together without ever coming into contact. At the end of the first chapter, the column of smoke seen by nearly everyone is the signal that the curtain has risen on the Jefferson stage.

CHARACTER ANALOGIES

The characters are linked by analogies which either draw them together because of their similarities or underline their differences. For instance, Joe and Lena, the opposite poles of the book, have nevertheless certain traits in common, similarities which make their differences the sharper. They are both orphans, both have left their families, setting out on their adventures through a window. Each has a love affair which ends in betrayal, and they both roam far and wide, the one in search of himself, the other in search of her seducer. On the other hand, the analogies between Joe and Hightower show that they are more alike than one would imagine. They share the same alienation from society and are both murderers: one has killed his mistress, the other has indirectly killed his wife. It is fitting that they should come together at the end. The futility of Hightower's attempt to save Joe does not detract from its importance as a sign recognizing their fraternity and showing that he has at last uncovered the secret of his wrecked life; his confession in the next chapter is a direct result of this. Similarly, the inclusion in the novel of Percy Grimm is justified by his resemblance to Christmas. A luminous angel in a church window, a clear-voiced young priest, Grimm shares a quality of ecstatic serenity with Joe, who is often likened to a monk or a choirboy. Like Christmas, Percy Grimm is a solitary man, desperately trying to gain admittance to a society from which he feels isolated. And he too is a murderer, of course. So it is fitting that both men should be pawns moved by the anonymous Player, and that their faces should merge together in Hightower's vision.

Hightower and Joanna also have some traits in common. They both live in seclusion, ostracized by society. They are both bound up in their traditions, Joanna in militant abolitionism and Hightower in the pointless glamor of the

Confederate cavalry; and both these traditions seem absurd and abstract, the first in its doctrinaire fanaticism, the second in its wasted romance. Each is locked in a religion which parodies the true spirit of piety. They are both sterile and represent perversions of the natural order as it manifests itself in normal sexuality and reproduction. Both ultimately destroy those with whom they live, by using them as a means to egoistic ends: in this context the fate of Hightower's wife anticipates Joe's own end.

Joe, too, has some similarity to Joanna, in their common isolation and intolerance. Moreover, Miss Burden was christened Joanna in memory of her father's first wife, Juana, a Mexican whom Grandfather Burden classed as a "nigger." Ironically, Joe, who had a supposedly Mexican father, and was classed as a "nigger" by Joanna, is probably no more so than her own half-brother, Calvin. Thus, Joanna reflects Joe, throwing back an image both similar and reverse: for while Joe has no identity and no family background, Joanna is entangled in family traditions which smother her identity.

For the purposes of the plot, Brown is not really a necessary character. That Lena should find him in Jefferson, where she gives birth to his son, savors strongly of contrivance. However, the coincidence is less blatant if Brown's role is to throw the other characters into relief. His betrayal of his responsibilities contrasts with Lena's acceptance of hers. But Brown, the "disciple," is most effective as an ironic double of Christmas, the "master" (p. 40). Brown is a white but he has dark skin, while Christmas, whose name suggests the light brought to the world, is considered a Negro. Mrs. Hines confuses Brown's son with the baby Joe, and deeper irony is achieved when she thinks that Christmas is really the father of the child. Such confusion becomes comical as Lena herself begins to believe her. Finally, when Brown was trying to escape without forfeiting the reward, it seemed to him that everyone, and even the money, were all like chessmen, moved about the board without reason by an "Opponent" who made up his own rules as he went along (p. 414). This symbol of fatality, which is later applied to Grimm's pursuit of Christmas, is thus first used of the disciple, Brown, and that in spite of the fact that it does not fit in with his character. The irony is followed through right to the end: Brown outwits the "Opponent" and manages to escape and lose his identity, while Christmas dies in a final attempt to assert his. In this way, Christmas's death is the tragical counterpoint of Brown's comical flight.

The difficulty in distinguishing between Hightower's and Miss Burden's ancestors points to calculated confusion between several characters. All the Burdens are called either Nathaniel or Calvin, and through three generations the Hightowers are referred to as "father" or "son" with no further definition. Moreover, there are many similarities between the two sets. Both families had a glorious past, and lived in relative harmony with their time, unlike the last representatives of the lines. The abolitionist tradition is coupled with fanaticism, and one is ready to kill for the cause, whether in private affairs or in the actual Civil War. Hightower bears the mark of his grandfather's absurd death, just as Miss Burden bears the mark of the murders of the two Calvins for the sake of a vote. As the ancestors of these two families remind the reader of the fanatics of the present, McEachern, Hines, and Grimm, and as Christmas himself carries on the tradition of violent intolerance, it would appear that Faulkner created the confusion deliberately. Thus, the import of the novel is not limited to one place, one era—the contemporary South—but extends to the eternal human condition in which persecutors and persecuted are forever interchangeable.

Finally, many of the male characters are alike in becoming father figures in relation to Christmas. John L. Longley has traced the similarities in the destinies of Oedipus and Christmas.[10] After causing the death of his true father,

Christmas is persecuted by the father figures, Doc Hines, McEachern, and Percy Grimm, and eventually one of them sacrifices and castrates him. Possibly, the masculine Joanna is an inverted and perverted version of the same figure. She certainly has the same fanaticism and the same belief in herself as a God-sent avenger: "Will you kneel with me? . . . I don't ask it. It's not I who ask it. Kneel with me" (p. 267). And *she* tries to kill Joe before he kills her. In the same context, the grandfathers of Joe, Hightower, and Joanna could be seen as images and envoys of God the Father, the Almighty.

So it is that the recurring scenes, the parallels, and the constant interplay of analogy and contrast give to the events and characters more than their intrinsic significance, and create between them the overall unity and meaning of the novel—which could not be achieved by the plots when considered as mere sequences of events.

CONTRAPUNTAL STRUCTURE

Thus it is reaffirmed that the unity of the work and its meaning are the direct results of the much-maligned changeovers from plot to plot. To talk of main plots and subplots in this context is a sign of having misunderstood their function. As early as 1935, James W. Linn and Houghton W. Taylor rightly spoke of counterpoint in relation to the structure of *Light in August*.[11] Lena Grove's story balances that of Joe Christmas, and Hightower's combines the two: Hightower actually meets both Lena and Christmas, although those two never meet each other. If the interest lay solely in the plot, that would be a flaw; but if the structure is the result of a balance between the plots and their opposed sets of values, then this is the ideal arrangement. That is why Faulkner shifts fairly regularly between the plots and their characters; this device is of course another way of creating suspense, as he has a remarkable talent for interrupting a plot at the right moment.[12] He even tries to interlock the three plots formally. At the beginning, the first chapter deals with Lena's calm confidence, the second with the threatening world of Christmas, the third with Hightower's life: at the end in almost reverse order, the last three chapters show, respectively, the pursuit and death of Christmas, Hightower's passion, and Lena's calm resumption of the journey interrupted by the birth of her child. The order of these last chapters finally confirms what the rest of the novel indicates—that Joe and Lena represent the poles of the novel and that Hightower is in an intermediary position, moving from one to the other. Although he is neither the most sympathetic nor the most closely examined of the characters, he nevertheless holds a central position in the overall economy of the novel. And the fact that Lena's story encloses the work at start and finish provides the norm, essential if the reader is to put Christmas's story into perspective. Cleanth Brooks justly makes this point, to the extent of paradoxically claiming that because of this predominance, *Light in August* must be a pastoral: "It is Lena and her instinct for nature, Lena and her rapport with the community, Lena as a link in the eternal progression from mother to daughter who provides the final norm for our judgement."[13] A study of the manuscript shows that Faulkner wished to accord her so much weight: originally the description of Hightower now in chapter 3 opened the book, but then Faulkner rearranged it so that the novel began and ended with Lena. (The short Texas manuscript, which precedes the Virginia manuscript, also began with Hightower.[14]) The fact that she is a comic figure does not in any way jeopardize her position since humor and comedy are the best media through which to cope with tragedy and horror. As for Faulkner, he was certainly not lacking in either humor or modesty when he gave this explanation of his ordering of the novel:

Unless a book follows a simple direct line such as a story of adventure, it becomes a series of pieces. It's a good deal like dressing a showcase window. It takes a certain amount of judgement and taste to arrange the different pieces in the most effective place in juxtaposition to one another.[15]

His art, as he was well aware, was of a different nature to that of a window dresser.

TENSES IN *LIGHT IN AUGUST*

The use of the tenses confirms the cohesion of the novel considered as a counterpoint of themes. It is partly inaccurate to say that the present is used for the ten days of the action in the present and the past for everything that came before; it would moreover neglect the author's intentions. Sometimes, it is true, it is difficult to explain a change of tense: for instance, in chapter 18 there seem to be no real reasons for tense changes, nor do they seem to suggest any special purpose on the author's part. Often, of course, a change of tense from present to past marks a flashback. There are sufficient examples of this in chapter 1 alone: since the novel opens on the picture of Lena sitting by the side of the road, on top of a hill as we learn later, everything which precedes this moment is of the past. Thus the sketch of her life up to this point (pp. 1-4), her sight of the wagon a mile before and of the two farmers squatting by a barn (p. 5), their discussion, and Armstid's departure until he is near enough to see Lena (pp. 6-8) are all in the past tense. However, anteriority does not explain every change of tense. It would seem that Faulkner has deliberately used the present tense to describe not only Lena—who, as a symbolic figure, has no past but inhabits a continual present—but also everything that relates to her and her values. In chapter 2 for example, he says of Byron: "Then Byron fell in love. He fell in love contrary to all the tradition of his austere and jealous country raising. . . . It happens on a Saturday afternoon while he is alone at the mill. Two miles away the house is still burning. . . . They saw it before noon . . . ," (p. 44). Then a discussion which took place in the morning is interpolated before the narration continues: "Lena Grove walked into the door behind him. . . . He hears her and turns and sees her face . . . ." (p. 45). While Faulkner is telling the parts of Byron's story which do not concern Lena, he uses the past tense: but as soon as Byron enters Lena's sphere and unknowingly falls in love with her, he adopts the present tense. Similarly, at the beginning of chapter 14 the discussion between the sheriff and his deputy is in the past until Lena becomes its subject.

This same intention on Faulkner's part is also patent in a study of the manuscript of the novel and of the salesman's dummy of the book. In the two-page text of that dummy, Lena's wait as the creaking wagon draws near is in the past: in both the manuscript and the published version, the corresponding passage is in the present. The text of the dummy is clearly a part of a first version of the novel, which can be traced in the manuscript. Indeed, Faulkner rewrote the first chapters, cutting out some parts of a previous version and pasting them onto the pages of the manuscript we know. The end of chapter 2, from Lena's entry into the shed at the planing mill, is taken from that first version, and all the verbs originally in the past have been altered to the present. On the other hand, there are several signs of indecision over tenses in chapter 1, with the conversation of the two farmers after Lena passes by (pp. 7–8) and the account of her journey with Armstid, whose view is then predominant (pp. 19–22), eventually being left in the past tense.

In contrast to Lena, Christmas is locked in his past and thus is always described in the past tense, except at the very end, when acceptance of his fate, perhaps only due to weariness or resignation, seems to bring him closer to Lena's world. So Faulkner has used tense changes for chronological differentiation, but also in an original way, to enhance the thematic structure of the novel. In answer to a question on this subject asked at the University of Virginia, Faulkner said: "that just seemed to me the best way to tell the story. It wasn't a deliberate change of style. I don't know anything about style."[16] He may have relished answering in this wise, but there is proof in the manuscript of *Light in August* that the changes of tense were the result of deliberate calculation.

TIME IN *LIGHT IN AUGUST*

Another key to the novel's meaning lies in its chronological disruption. Faulkner rarely follows the conventional temporal order since the distinctions between past, present, and future do not exist for him. The past is the only real dimension of time—or rather the reemergence of the past into the present. The present is woven from the thread of the past, not remembered as memories, but actually lived as destiny since it is already written: "time is a fluid condition which has no existence except in the momentary avatars of individual people. There is no such thing as *was*—only *is*."[17] This is precisely what—in Faulkner's own words—Christmas experiences before committing the crime he thinks he has already committed, as temporal distinctions do not exist: "The dark was filled with the voices, myriad, out of all time that he had known, as though all the past was a flat pattern. And going on: tomorrow night, all the tomorrows, to be a part of the flat pattern, going on . . . since tomorrow to-be and had-been would be the same" (p. 266).[18] The lack of punctuation in the last part of this sentence makes clear Faulkner's intention.

Such a view of time shows that the concept of memory as such does not exist for Faulkner, since memory cannot re-create an incident of the past with all the qualities of the vanished time. A memory is re-created by a mind in the present and so shot across with the actual circumstances in which it is recalled that it becomes a new experience. Miss Rosa explains this to Quentin in *Absalom, Absalom!* (p. 143): *"there is no such thing as memory: the brain recalls just what the muscles grope for: no more, no less: and its resultant sum is usually incorrect and false and worthy only of the name of dream."* Faulkner refers to this phenomenon at the beginning of chapter 6 in *Light in August:* "Memory believes before knowing remembers. Believes longer than recollects, longer than knowing even wonders." This means that memory is the intuition of a being who sees himself as the sum of his experiences—the significance of which is not apparent until an instant in the present recalls them into being; it is an assertion of the continuity of existence, an intimate adherence to a past become destiny even though it disappears into subconsciousness or oblivion ("Believes longer than recollects"). Christmas is in precisely this state of mind when he kills Joanna. In view of this, one should not reproach Faulkner (as sometimes has been done) for the imbalance of the account of Christmas's life, where great stress is laid on some experiences of his childhood and adolescence, whereas the fifteen years he spent wandering along an endless street are almost totally ignored. The thirty-six-year-old man who feels one August night that something is going to happen to him knows ("Memory believes") that the present moment is the result of some, and only some, of the experiences which have left lifelong marks on him.

Together chapters 6–12 provide the most remarkable demonstration of this conception of time in the book. But there are plenty of other examples elsewhere in the novel and within the fabric of these six chapters. In the very first chapter the flashback into Lena's life (pp. 1–4) avoids introducing in the past tense a character who is essentially of the present. Faulkner has even succeeded in creating the impression, at the beginning of the flashback, that it is part of Lena's thoughts: the words "Doane's Mill" cross her present thoughts and are immediately taken up at the beginning of the flashback, conjuring up not the orderly memories of her life (Faulkner later arranges them as he does Christmas's), but a precise image and emotion associated with her shoes. So Faulkner builds certain of his flashbacks around key words or images charged with special emotion for the characters. This tactic enables him to curtail his narration of the past without depriving it of its original emotional impact. Thus, he summarizes Lena's memories around the image of the window. Similarly, Christmas's life of wandering is circumscribed by the image of the street, and his relationship with Joanna by a few words and images at the beginning of chapter 11: first, "to tell" and "to talk," then in the second paragraph, "to see," in the third, "to stand" and "to sit," and in the fourth the image of the thief. In chapter 8 the story goes back four or five years (pp. 173–74) because the memory of Joe's first date with Bobbie is for him irrevocably linked with a particular feeling of physical unease and repulsion: on that occasion he vomited in the woods. As soon as the memory of this meeting is stimulated, before he can even recall the precise day, he is led back automatically to the first time he experienced the same sensation for the same reasons: once a boy had told him about menstruation in terms which had an ineradicable effect on him: "a picture, physical, actual, to be discerned by the sense of smell and even of sight" (p. 173).

Even these few examples suffice to show that Faulkner takes so little account of chronological order in recounting a character's life because he abides by the current of the individual's psychic life. The same experience will always be linked with the same sensations and will return to the memory when prompted by the recurrence of the sensation. A chronological account of events would strip them of their original force and power of suggestion, since such an arrangement separates them from their accompanying emotion, and makes them lose the fourth dimension, that of physical sensation or emotion. Where the linear, chronological account ends at a given juncture, an account according to memory, going from effect to cause instead of from cause to effect, starts at that juncture and re-creates the event in its full immediacy. Alain Resnais uses a similar technique in *L'année dernière à Marienbad* and in *Je t'aime, je t'aime.*

It is only because of this temporal dislocation that the author can so easily fill in the characters' past, without which their present would be incomprehensible. About Lena there is very little to understand: hence, apart from the first few pages, which are indispensable for the reader, her life is followed chronologically. It is different for Christmas. Although the first four chapters go from the past and his arrival in Jefferson to the present, the Sunday evening after the murder, from chapter 5 onward Faulkner gradually works into Joe's past. He starts with the day before the murder in chapter 5, then moves to his remembered life in chapters 6–12, and finally to his existence from birth and even conception in chapter 16. The diagram is similar for Hightower. Thus, these characters would seem to be presented through two opposite movements: the reader goes further and further into their past while they move nearer to their perfectly foreseeable crises. So, since the issue is already known, this return to the past acts as a step-by-step revelation of destiny.

However, to see *Light in August* as an anti-detective novel because the solutions are revealed so early shows only partial appreciation of the writer's intentions. For the novel is a real inquiry, but into the understanding of the facts rather than into the facts themselves: "It is in this understanding, not in the actual succession of events, that Faulkner places the climax of interest."[19] As a result, events and characters are often kept in suspension until one is given the wherewithal to understand them. For instance, in chapter 4 it is said that Christmas has black blood in him: the revelation, whether true or false, hardly affects the superficial knowledge of him gained so far. As Joe's life is gradually revealed, however, this detail gains in importance until it eventually seems to be the key which could unlock the problem of his whole existence. The significance of his black blood becomes psychological rather than physiological, and that is why Faulkner leaves its truth uncertain. Particularly after Joanna's narrative, the supposed black blood collects about it a mass of symbolic connotations. Yet it is not until the end, when it spurts forth, raising Joe into a symbolic ascension, that these connotations are fully developed, even though this conclusion remains ambiguous. Faulkner's brand of suspense is exactly this state of uncertainty, which is only made possible by the temporal dislocation. The brilliant success of his most complex novel, *Absalom, Absalom!*, is due to a systematic application of this technique to its characters and, even more, to its facts.

CONCLUSION

Light in August is not what might be called a faultless novel. Certain passages do not seem quite necessary, distracting the reader from the main drift of the work. There would also seem to be some indecision in the disposition of the chapters: the plots alternate or enclose one another at the beginning of the book and after chapter 13, but chapters 5–12 are devoted exclusively to Christmas's story. That is because at the end of chapter 4 Faulkner was faced with a choice of two directions. He had to attempt an explanation of Christmas's murder of Joanna, which involved going deeply into Joe's past, and he also had to follow Hightower and motivate his reluctant and painful move from one set of values to another. Faulkner dealt with the former first and then concentrated on the second after chapter 13. He does, it is true, carry on with Christmas's story at the same time, but now he is seen from a distance,

through other characters and particularly through Hightower. The latter becomes the reverberator of the second
half of the novel, like Horace Benbow in *Sanctuary*.

Several times Faulkner has explained how *The Sound
and the Fury* developed from a mental picture of the muddy
seat of a little girl's drawers, in a pear tree, where she
could watch her grandmother's funeral through a window.
When he did not succeed in telling this little girl's story
through Benjy, he had to try again repeatedly in other
sections of the book. *Light in August* was apparently similarly
developed from the image of the pregnant Lena traveling
on a road; it is therefore suitable that this view of her
should begin and end the book: "that story began with
Lena Grove, the idea of the young girl with nothing,
pregnant, determined to find her sweetheart. It was . . .
out of my admiration for women, for the courage and
endurance of women. As I told that story I had to get
more and more into it, but that was mainly the story of
Lena Grove."[20]

So it appears that Christmas and Hightower were originally introduced only so that Faulkner could tell the story
of Lena. Now these two, and especially Christmas, are so
fully developed that they take up most of the novel. It
seems that Lena was rather created at a later date to be
the antithesis of Christmas, when in fact it was the other
way round. Faulkner's characters are indeed so alive for
him that they sometimes assume more importance than
he intended; and they may even escape him altogether
and, as we have seen, tempt him away from his principal
objective. That is why it is difficult to say categorically
which is the protagonist. Lena may have been the germ
of the novel and remain its alpha and omega, and Christmas
may be the most absorbing character (the six chapters devoted to his life are among Faulkner's best), but Hightower,
in spite of his flaws and shortcomings, is the moral center.

Thus it seems as though Faulkner had no consistent

design throughout the novel. But then, could it be otherwise? He had to try to reconcile two apparently contradictory intentions: following the three plots and outwardly connecting them to one another, and going beyond the interest of each individual intrigue so that the full meaning of the novel would naturally arise from their combination and from their thematic and contrapuntal interdependence. Yet was not the realization of both intentions a well-nigh impossible ambition? A few years later, in *The Wild Palms,* Faulkner again used the same technique; but it is significant that the two plots of this "double novel" are linked only thematically, not factually. *Light in August* may then appear to have been an overambitious undertaking. However, is it not the attempt to achieve the impossible which gives a work its grandeur? Faulkner himself expressed this view in several interviews, when he was asked to give his opinion of his contemporaries and of himself:

All of us failed to match our dream of perfection. So I rate us on the basis of our splendid failure to do the impossible.

To try something you can't do, because it's too much [to hope for], but still to try it and fail, then try it again. That to me is success. [21]

3

The Characters

"Paradox" is a word dear to Faulkner, and could well be used to sum up the impression left by the characters. None of those in *Light in August* are described in detail, and they are at times barely visualized apart from a few sketched lines. They remain physically "flat" in spite of pregnancies or protruding stomachs, and hardly seem to exist on a physical plane. Nevertheless, they are undeniably real and immediately insinuate themselves into the reader's imagination, to the point of becoming obsessively present. For Faulkner, with no idea of creating a realistic or sociological novel, dwells less on the material than on the spiritual aspects, less on the appearance than on the being, a method which does not give rise to three-dimensional creations. Thus, even though he sometimes resorts to traditional techniques, his character drawing is basically highly individual, the expression of a mental vision. Such a vision, too, dictates the narrative technique and the contrapuntal structure, making possible the confrontation of two antithetical worlds, which are also, as we shall see, reflected in the shades of light strikingly characterizing the landscape.

The simplification, or rather stylization, of the characters is apparent in the special vocabulary connected with each one, in the brief descriptions of their appearance, and also, to a lesser degree, in their immobilization. They are not types, however, hieratic abstractions, simple mouthpieces. Faulkner contrives to give them physical presence by giving their sensations a forceful immediacy, and by describing them simultaneously from the outside and from the inside, thereby blurring the differences between the voices of the characters and that of the author. The physical details are replaced by abstract qualities, impressions or, better, expressions of a personal vision, giving the characters greater malleability and allowing the author to model them more easily, to enlarge them, to make them bear a significance greater than would be warranted by their physical stature. He achieves this by immobilizing them at given times, and also by associating them, fairly fluidly, with certain myths. It is remarkable that while Faulkner's technique indubitably creates somewhat stylized characters, they are not for all that simplified or abstract: on the contrary, they remain alive, often inexplicable and ambiguous, and are even made larger than life by his art.

CHARACTERS AND VOCABULARY

Faulkner reduces his characters to a few essential, not incidental or temporary, qualities by repeatedly using for each one a certain number of key words or images. A character's presence becomes so inextricably connected with these words or images that they eventually carry the whole personality, take the very color of obsessions, rages, or outrages, and evoke the character without his even being named.

This technique is perfectly illustrated by the minor and therefore less complex characters. A hard life and five children have given Mrs. Armstid her sharp angles, her brusque impatience, which Faulkner transposes into a few well-chosen, oft-repeated words: "gray," "busy," "cold," "hard," and the variations "manhard" and "workhard." Most often he resorts to the adjective "savage," which he has used already of Armstid (p. 10): "the gray woman . . .

manhard, workhard, in a serviceable gray garment worn savage and brusque"; "Mrs. Armstid at the stove clashes the metal lids . . . with the abrupt savageness of a man"; "She clashes the stove savagely"; "She is still busy at the stove. It appears to require an amount of attention out of all proportion to the savage finality with which she built the fire"; "a savage screw of gray hair at the base of her skull" (pp.14–15). The first and fourth of these quotations are not included in the manuscript, showing that when Faulkner corrected and typed out the text he did not want to add further details to his portrait, but sought rather to underline and strengthen its characterizing traits. Twice more "gray," "hard," and "savage" are used, and "busy" and "brusque" also entrench their position. As "savage" (or its derivatives) appears five times in little more than a page, and is used indiscriminately to describe Mrs. Armstid's clothes, her screw of hair, and her movements, the word asserts itself as qualifying and representing the whole person, not just the relevant portion. In this way, concrete, visual details give way to abstract impressions which suggest the essence of the person. The abstract eventually becomes that person's substance, giving an impression of unreality which is in fact surrealistic. A few pages later, when Mrs. Armstid breaks open her china bank, the word "savage" recurs twice with variants ("violently," "harsh," and even "bitter"): the reader already associates this impatient sharpness with her even in her generous gestures, thanks to that word and its variations, overtones of the fundamental note.

An examination of other minor characters would bring similar conclusions. For instance, in chapter 6 the janitor of the orphanage is described as a dirty little man with mad eyes and voice. In chapter 15 the words "dirty" and "crazy" and their variants immediately reveal him to be Doc Hines. His vocabulary, too, identifies him tellingly, with the recurrence of those striking compound words which condense in a single form his identification of Woman and sin. When "a little, dirty old man with a short goat's beard who seemed to be in a state like catalepsy" appears on the station platform (p. 420), he is straightaway recognized as that crazy satyr whose sensuality has turned into a physical hatred of Woman. Similarly, Mame is created in only two images and their variants, "brasshaired," ("brassridged hair," "violenthaired") and "diamondsurfaced respectability" (pp. 163, 164, 165, 204, 209). These expressions give no realistic description but they try to break through to the essential characteristics of this being, or rather of this type. Bobbie is characterized seven times by the word "downlooking," which is even used of her voice (pp. 175, 182), so that it seems to be less a facial position than the total attitude and circumstance of a woman who is at the mercy of men's cupidity and desires. In the first description of McEachern, everything conspires to paint the same picture of a hard, immovable man, apparently devoid of sentiment. Thereafter, this flawless quality of hardness is easily evoked by the use of "rocklike" (pp. 135, 138, 149, 191) or "granitelike" (p. 143), or a few striking images for his head: "the indomitable bullet head" (p. 217), "one of the marble cannon balls on Civil War monuments" (p. 153). Brown, too, is reduced to a single characteristic, his subhuman inanity. Faulkner continually suggests that he has elements of the mechanical and the animal, by comparing him to any one of a menagerie of mules, horses, grasshoppers, snakes, rats, or any frightened or fleeing animal, or by stressing his empty, spasmodic movements: "scattered," "erratic," and especially "jerking." He even goes so far as to liken him to a car "running along the street with a radio in it," going nowhere "in particular and when you look at it close you see that there ain't even anybody in it" (pp. 32–33).

A reading of chapter 1 and the second part of chapter 2 supplies all the key words associated with Lena. They gradually combine to reduce Lena to the single quality of serenity. The adjective "serene" makes the use of her name unnecessary when she enters Byron's workshop (p. 45). A few lines later Faulkner decided to use the same adjective again, although he used "placid" in the manuscript. This quality shows in her tranquil doggedness, her seeming detachment—she is apparently enclosed in a dreamlike eternal present where day-to-day occurrences pass her by, and leave her unruffled— and also in the light which seems to emanate from within her ("inwardlighted," p. 15; "that inward listening deliberation," p. 12), giving her both her transparency and her warmth.

Even before we know anything of Christmas, Faulkner suggests in chapter 2 what the man is capable of by using the image of the snake three times (pp. 29, 35, 41). He also uses certain adjectives suggestive of his future actions (just as Hawthorne treats Chillingworth): "dark," "baleful," "arrogant," "contemptuous," "cold." He refers to his parchment-colored skin, "as though the skull had been . . . baked in a fierce oven" (p. 30), the visible sign of burning experiences, as for Captain Ahab.[1] But the menacing, fatal atmosphere which hangs around him is only one aspect of the character. Above all, Christmas is a wanderer, rootless, as the first description testifies: "He looked like a tramp, yet not like a tramp either" (p. 27). The contradiction of the two statements shows that Faulkner wishes to reach the center of the person through his appearances: the first part of the sentence on its own would have given only the appearance and implied that this was the reality. In typing the text Faulkner stressed this spiritual rootlessness by adding: "there was something definitely rootless about him, as though no town nor city was his, no street, no walls, no square of earth his home. And that he carried his knowledge with him always as though it were a banner, with a quality ruthless, lonely, and almost proud" (p. 27). This addition has the double function of already associating Christmas with the obsessive image of the street, and of reducing him to one significant quality, his rootlessness, his searching, not for a home but for an identity. His spiritual wandering is the essence of his character and his "banner," identifying him as surely as if it were a mask in Greek tragedy. The idea is confirmed by another image frequently used of Joe, that of the ghost or shade: "In the wide, empty, shadowbrooded street he looked like a phantom, a spirit, strayed out of its own world, and lost" (p. 106; cf. pp. 111, 112, 148, 175, 216). When Joanna applies it to the whole Negro race (p. 239) the image acquires its full force, for it is the uncertainty of whether this is his race or not that tortures Christmas.

Thus Faulkner contrives to reduce his characters to their essential elements: like Hawthorne, he tries to grasp the being through the appearance. For both of them, the latter is symptomatic of the former, as is said of Brown, "telling everybody who he was . . . in a tone and manner that was the essence of the man himself" (p. 33). Faulkner's characters, like Hawthorne's, are built around a small number of key words, often abstract, which represent and evoke them, and around a system of transposition, as both authors use metaphors and analogies freely to translate the invisible realities into visual impressions. Faulkner also uses a great many negative words (chapter 1 provides plenty of examples) with which he tries to pierce beyond the incidental and the ephemeral by contradicting the first impression, thereby giving his characters a depth and an aura of mystery which the words associated with them cannot supply. For those of his characters who run the risk of becoming types, or allegorical figures like Chillingworth and Pearl in *The Scarlet Letter,* this is a way of avoiding the danger.

PHYSICAL ASPECT OF THE CHARACTERS

The physical descriptions in spite of their cursory nature, are another aid in avoiding the danger of creating character

types. Faulkner's characters are two-dimensional, somewhat
like his early sketches published at the University of Mississippi in *Ole Miss* and *The Scream*[2] between 1917 and 1925,
but immediately recognizable because of a few simple stressed
traits. The word "silhouette" is frequently used in the
descriptions of characters who seem, says Faulkner, to be
cut out of cardboard, or as in the case of Popeye in *Sanctuary*
or Ab Snopes in "Barn Burning," out of tin. Christmas
is always easily recognizable, dressed in a white shirt and
dark trousers, a symbolic uniform, and wearing, like Popeye,
a straw hat slanted over a baleful face glimpsed through
the smoke rising from the inevitable cigarette. Lena's carriage
is equally constant and characteristic: she has a swollen
belly and the serene slowness of a pregnant woman, and,
like Christmas, she has her uniform and a few distinctive
attributes. Her clothes are of a pale, faded blue, she carries
a palm leaf fan, her few possessions make a small bundle
wrapped in a bandanna handkerchief, and she wears men's
shoes, which she often carries in her hand to go barefoot
through the soft dust. Hightower's clothes are shapeless
and dubious, and his sweaty, ill-washed and flabby flesh
seems already in a state of decay, as befits the half-dead
man he is. At once gaunt and swollen, he sags: "his upper
body in shape is like a loosely filled sack falling from
his gaunt shoulders of its own weight, upon his lap" (p.
72); his flaccid obesity suggests some monstrous pregnancy
(p. 291).

Often Faulkner prefers not to give an easily recognizable
outline of a character, but instead concentrates on one
particular feature which becomes, under this scrutiny, bizarre, monstrous, or nightmarish. This one detail stands
for and evokes the whole person, like Mame's hair, Bobbie's
hands, which are much too large for her childish frame,
and Brown's little white scar, which is likened to a slick
of saliva or a popcorn, and which becomes a telltale index
to his emotions (p. 406). Then there is Hightower's vast,

sagging paunch, or his immobile bust, an apt image of a man who has cut himself off from all life.

THE EYES

The eyes, more than any other feature, can embrace the whole of a character. Faulkner does not try to describe them, but to transpose into often unexpected images and analogies the essential traits which a character's eyes reveal. He says how he sees them rather than what they are like, re-creating them from the elements of his own vision by an expressionist technique. The matron of the orphanage is only described by her weak, kind, frustrated eyes (p. 124), which set like jelly when she realizes that she must put Joe into a white family (pp. 126, 133). The sheriff, too, is only concretized by his eyes, where all his acuteness is concentrated: "the fat man, with little wise eyes like bits of mica embedded in his fat, still face" (p. 398). The eyes of the Negro girl in the shed were like dead stars, dead like everything else connected with sexuality in this novel: Bobbie's eyes too are "without depth, as if they could not even reflect" (p. 169). McEachern's "stare cold and intent and yet not deliberately harsh" (p. 133) sums up the first description of him. Brown's eyes are miniatures of his whole bearing: while the sheriff questions him after the murder, his eyes dart from side to side, with the same robotlike jerkiness which stamps all his movements (pp. 90, 92); when he feels trapped in the cabin with Lena, his eyes are "like two terrified beasts," an apt simile for a man most often likened to an animal.

It is also through the eyes that understanding or the lack of it between the characters is shown. In *Light in August,* and even more in *As I Lay Dying,* the characters communicate with, or challenge, each other more through exchanged glances than in the spoken word. That is why the verb "to watch" recurs constantly in Faulkner. The real conversation between Mrs. Armstid and Lena, as they both well know, is held through their eyes: "They look at one another, suddenly naked, watching one another" (p. 15). When Christmas enters the planer shed he watches the other workers and holds them silent, hypnotized in his gaze, just as Popeye imprisons Benbow and the whole space around the spring in his unmoving stare at the beginning of *Sanctuary*. In the same shed Lena watches Byron and literally holds him prisoner ("to watch" occurs here over and over again), until he has told her, unwittingly, all about her seducer; and Byron is aware of the fixity of her gaze, which seems to deprive him temporarily of his faculty of judgment (pp. 50, 72). Joe's awareness of his difference from the others at the orphanage and forever afterwards is largely due to Hines's persistent watching of him, locking him in the circle from which he will never be able to escape: *"That is why I am different from the others: because he is watching me all the time"* (p. 129). Thus, just as a snake fascinates its prey, Faulkner's characters sometimes seem to hold those they watch inside their gaze. Hightower's mother is an extreme case: when Hightower was a child he felt that his whole existence was bound within her eyes: "he thought of her . . . as being only that thin face and the two eyes which seemed daily to grow bigger and bigger, as though about to embrace all seeing, all life, . . . he could feel them through all walls. They were the house: he dwelled within them . . ." (pp. 449–50).

The emphasis laid on the eyes, so prominent in all Faulkner's novels, is one instance of the technique of stressing one part of a character. This one part, in each case enlarged, deformed, or remodeled by the author's idea of it, takes the place of the whole character, and it is its bizarre or monstrous quality which fixes itself on the reader's mind. Faulkner's characters are truly the projection, the expression of a mental image.

3 · THE CHARACTERS

IMMEDIACY

Although they are stylized, reduced to the essence, even deformed, the characters are not lifeless abstracts, puppets used as mouthpieces or implemented to concretize ideas or obsessions. On the contrary, they are indubitably—and paradoxically—actual, endowed with a concrete existence, imposing themselves upon the reader whether he wishes it or not. This is largely due to Faulkner's gift of giving immediacy to their sensations. It is true that they sometimes seem detached, observing their own movements, although this does not mean that they can control them, for they are more often powerless before the events which overtake them. Quite often, however, they are incapable of taking a clear objective view of themselves. In these circumstances, Faulkner describes their sensations instantaneously, with no explanations, creating the impression that they are totally ensnared by their experiences. The reader is thus deprived of the possibility of reconstructing their sensations intellectually and organizing them into reassuring perceptions; he is forced to share the characters' experiences by empathy.

This is very evident in the Dewey Dell sections in *As I Lay Dying*, and in the pages in *Sanctuary* covering the twenty-four hours spent by Temple at Frenchman's Bend, where one feels the simultaneous growth of her terror and fascination. There are numerous examples in Joe's life story too. An excellent one is the moment when he leaves the restaurant "sweating the half-dollar," swept away upon the laughing of the patrons (p. 172). And when Brown tells how, when he discovered Joe's nightly visits to the Burden house, he first laughed, and then stopped suddenly, his account does not follow a logical order, but the order of emotional response:

Christmas struck a match. Then Brown said he quit laughing and he laid there and watched Christmas light the lantern and set it on the box by Brown's cot. Then Brown said how he wasn't laughing and he laid there and Christmas standing there by the cot, looking down at him (p. 87).

His surprise and apprehension when Christmas strikes a match are so great that he can neither analyze nor even name their cause, which was presumably the look on Joe's face. He can only give the effect—that he stopped laughing—which he mentions twice. Now this is how Lena appears to Armstid when he stops his wagon near her: "From beneath a sunbonnet of faded blue, . . . she looks up at him quietly and pleasantly: young, pleasantfaced . . ." (p. 9). But in the manuscript the sentence reads: "She looks quietly and pleasantly up at Armstid from beneath the sunbonnet of faded blue." Faulkner obviously changed the word order so that he could stress "pleasant" by repetition, and also, more importantly, follow Armstid's own perception of her. Finally, many of Faulkner's characters experience synesthetic sensations, which give a startling effect of immediacy: *"I smelling my mouth and tongue weeping the hot salt of waiting my eyes tasting the hot steam from the dish"* (p. 217). In this way Faulkner prevents the reader's setting himself apart from the characters, forcing him to share their sensations rather than judge them. It is significant that Gavin Stevens, who wishes to understand everything in rational terms, only grasps an abstraction, not a living person. The reason cannot comprehend the movements of the heart, whose qualities—often summed up by the word "compassion"—are more important than those of the intellect. That is surely what Lena teaches us.

Sometimes the narrative technique reinforces the immediacy, as, in moments of dramatic stress, it slides from indirect to direct presentation. This is illustrated, for instance, in chapter 4, when Byron arrives at Mrs. Beard's (p. 17), and during the interrogation, when, feeling himself trapped, Brown reveals that Christmas is probably of mixed blood (p. 89).

THE VOICE

Faulkner often uses his characters' own voices in narration, or, more frequently still, gives the impression that it is they who are speaking even though they are described from outside, a technique which endows them with life and actuality. In fact, the distinction is often blurred between the dramatization of a character's inner consciousness and the narration or description by an omniscient author. Faulkner merges these two methods, traditional narration and stream of consciousness, and so creates an intermediate voice with a tone completely its own. Thus he will describe a character from the outside, while reproducing the different levels of the character's own voice so that the narration always seems to be in the various tones of that same voice. Some modern musicians record a variety of sounds and then modulate and amplify these raw materials to produce a unique and personal whole, in which the original sounds are more or less recognizable. In the same way, the reader sometimes does hear the voices of Lena, Byron, or, more rarely, Joe, but at other times the pitch of their voices is so modified and amplified as to sound very like the author's. Yet Faulkner's fingertip control never allows the impression that one is at the center of the character's consciousness to be destroyed. This technique is more delicate than the one used in Benjy's section of *The Sound and the Fury,* where the voice is always of the same intensity.

In conversations or when a character thinks aloud—when Faulkner uses double quotation marks—the voice is clearly that of the character. His own expressions and pronunciation are respected, and the intensity of the speaker's voice is consistent.

Sometimes a character formulates his thoughts clearly, using his own vocabulary, and his voice is then recognizable even though he is not speaking aloud. The thought is then in single quotation marks and is usually introduced or followed by "thinks" or "thinking." One example suffices to show an intermediary level of amplification and how conscious Faulkner was of the suppleness of the technique: "[Armstid] says to himself, between thinking and saying aloud: 'I reckon she will. I reckon that fellow is fixing to find that he made a bad mistake when he stopped this side of Arkansas, or even Texas'" (p. 11).

Often, though, a character's thoughts are semi-conscious, simultaneous with action or actual speech. Then they are usually printed in italics and introduced by "thinking," without quotation marks or final punctuation. But they are not necessarily in the character's idiom: it is his voice, but not his style, as Faulkner transcends and formulates his most fleeting thoughts at their instant of conception, when they are probably more striking than when they have been pondered and put into the character's own words. The author thus expresses evanescent thoughts, which are too swiftly come and gone for the character himself to grasp them:

> Then [Joe] looked at [the heifer], and it was again too fast and too complete to be thinking: *That is not a gift. It is not even a promise: it is a threat* thinking, 'I didn't ask for it. He gave it to me. I didn't ask for it,' believing *God knows, I have earned it* [pp. 170–71]

> Perhaps he had already expected some fateful mischance, thinking, 'It was too good to be true, anyway'; thinking too fast for even thought: *In a moment she will vanish. She will not be. And then I will be back home, in bed, not having left it at all* Her voice went on: "I forgot about the day of the month when I told you Monday night." [p. 176]

These two examples demonstrate Faulkner's skilful variation of intensity or tone. The following extract clearly shows how the character's voice merges with the author's as the original thought is gradually amplified. Joe, aged seventeen, remembers the waitress he saw a few months before:

> 'I dont even know what they are saying to her,' he thought, thinking *I dont even know that what they are saying to her is*

something that men do not say to a passing child believing I do not know yet that in the instant of sleep the eyelid closing prisons within the eye's self her face demure, pensive; tragic, sad, and young; waiting, colored with all the vague and formless magic of young desire. [p. 165]

Sometimes Faulkner even says that he expresses in his own voice and words what a character thinks but is unable to say. This does help somehow to preserve the illusion that it is the character's voice:

If the child had been older he would perhaps have thought *He hates me and fears me. So much so that he cannot let me out of his sight* With more vocabulary but no more age he might have thought *That is why I am different from the others: because he is watching me all the time* [p. 129]

Finally, the ultimate stage of amplification is used to concretize what is latent and unexpressed in a character's mind. In chapters 6–12, though a framework is set up and recalled again from time to time (variations on "memory" and "knowing"), the narration is that of an omniscient author, and the chapters concerning Joe's life seem little different from say chapter 20, Hightower's confession. In fact, the difference is stylistic not technical. Faulkner adapts his style to the gradually revealed character in each case; and Hightower and Joe require very different styles. One of Faulkner's achievements in *Light in August* is indeed his way of seeming to present a character from the inside, creating the illusion that the story springs from the character and is a continuation of his voice, even though the description may in fact be objective and external. He does it through vocabulary and tone, not through technique as such.

The advantages of this technique are obvious. The style can be varied without losing its unity. Faulkner has the best of both worlds: by amplifying all the vague, fleeting, latent, or forgotten thoughts of a character without being restrained by the latter's limited intelligence or consciousness, he gives the reader the impression that he participates in that character's life. He retains the emotional force of a subjective account while giving it the fullness and fluency of an objective one. Since a voice thus modulated seems at once external and internal to the character, both emanating from him and enveloping him, a three-dimensional effect not unlike that of stereophonic sound is produced.

MOVEMENT AND IMMOBILITY

We have seen how Faulkner gives his characters their life and actuality. He uses yet another method, more original and more remarkable, to convey the sense of their movements and to show the intensity of their psychic life. For Faulkner it is more than just another way of presenting his characters. It goes beyond their physical presence to give them greater stature and significance.

Paradoxically, Faulkner often renders movement by arresting it. The paradox is only superficial, however, for the suspension of a movement at its peak of speed or violence gives the arrested (but not stationary) image the added force of potential movement. The same effect is achieved in a film, when movement is suddenly frozen, giving the spectator the impression of greater restrained force. To the same end, Faulkner also renders movements in slow motion so that, again as in a film, a gesture becomes pure movement. While a movement restricted to its natural duration in time dies in stillness, a movement artificially suspended is freed from its time limits and is infinitely dynamic. Painting and sculpture, by their nature, must attempt to recapture movement and enclose it in a limited area and volume. Faulkner's early interest in drawing is not without significance in this context; he also frequently compares his characters' movements to those in pictures or sculpture, especially equestrian statues—in which the sculptor's art consists in imprisoning movement in solid form.[3]

The description of Joanna Burden in the throes of nymphomania provides a good illustration of this aspect of Faulkner's art (p. 245). The motions of her sexual delirium are slowed down almost into immobility, so that they appear more violent and irrepressible: "wild" recurs four times in that description. Details like the clothes torn to shreds or the "slow shifting from one to another of . . . formally erotic attitudes" savor of the artist's studio. The reference to Beardsley, who influenced Faulkner in his own drawings and who is already mentioned in *Soldiers' Pay*, supports this impression. Crazed with desire, Joanna gradually becomes immobilized by art as a portrait of nymphomania, or an allegorical Erotic Delirium. Now it can be seen that this technique does not merely render in words movement and violence: it also gives the character a larger, timeless dimension bordering on the mythical. The allusion to the author of *Satyricon* in this passage is no longer surprising, nor is the veiled reference to snaky-haired Medusa totally unexpected. Arrested in her frenzy, Joanna assumes an air of supernatural malevolence which she would not otherwise have. Beyond her nymphomania, one senses the archetype of evil, of which Joanna is but an "avatar" (the word is used in the previous paragraph). Joe's inability to resist this corrupting force, his terror on the edge of the abyss, and his compulsion to crime are thus better explained.

Numerous comparisons to sculpture may be found in Faulkner's work. There are several very fine ones in *As I Lay Dying*, when Jewel struggles with his horse, or when Gillespie tries to stop him from entering the flame-drenched barn. In *Light in August*, when Joe goes back to town on the horse of the man he has just knocked down, the exhausted beast moves more and more slowly, but the illusion of continual movement is preserved: "It—the horse and rider—had a strange, dreamy effect, like a moving picture in slow motion as it galloped steady and flagging up the street" (p. 196). It is precisely when movement ceases that the illusion of movement is best achieved, and that the sculptural image appears almost as a matter of course: "Yet still the rider leaned forward in the arrested saddle, in the attitude of terrific speed, . . . they might have been an equestrian statue strayed from its pedestal . . ." (p. 197). Outrage, which is contained rage or arrested violence, makes some characters take on statuesque properties, and their faces become masklike. Mame reminds one of "a carved lioness guarding a portal" (p. 164) or a bronze figure, Mrs. Armstid's face "might have been carved in sandstone" (p. 15), the granitelike McEachern's is as hard as sculpted stone (p. 141), and when Joe stonily refuses the food offered him by his foster mother, he too becomes statuelike (p. 145). The dietitian, when a prey to fury and terror, is likened to a tragic "aching mask in a fixed grimace of dissimulation that dared not flag" (p. 115). Even Brown's face, distorted in a paroxysm of rage, appropriately becomes an animal mask, "a spent and vulpine mask" (p. 413). Finally, when Hightower's future wife savagely talks to him of marriage, her face, which he then sees for the first time as belonging to a human being, paradoxically resembles a mask (p. 455).

These frequent and almost systematic mask analogies serve to transcribe physical and emotional movements by arresting them at their crisis. Their quality of statue- or canvas-like immobility renders them immemorial—one of Faulkner's favorite words—and suggests their relevance as eternal human verities, beyond actual experience. As we shall see, the myths Faulkner associates with his characters serve this purpose too, among others.

Faulkner obviously finds the conjunction of movement and immobility so fascinating a technique that he also uses it in showing his characters' relationship to their surroundings. Sometimes he transfers the movement of a character to the environment in which he moves. An ever moving character thus appears to be stationary while the countryside slides past in an equivalent movement. Joe does not flee in the same street for fifteen years, it flees beneath his feet, which illusion serves to strengthen the feeling of isolation, abandon, and powerlessness: "the street ran on in its moods and phases, always empty: he might have seen himself as in numberless avatars, in silence, doomed with motion, driven by the courage of flagged and spurred despair" (p. 213). Percy Grimm gives the same impression when he pursues Christmas with "the implacable undeviation of Juggernaut or Fate" (p. 435). In her journey from Alabama, Lena Grove seems to remain still while the road and the days draw out in her trail: "backrolling now behind her a long monotonous succession of peaceful and undeviating changes from day to dark and dark to day again, through which she advanced in identical and anonymous and deliberate wagons as though through a succession of creakwheeled and limpeared avatars, like something moving forever and without progress across an urn" (p. 5).

This transference of motion gives Faulkner's descriptions a dreamlike or nightmarish quality which does not, however, lead to unreality. On the contrary, it suggests a more profound (another favorite word) reality, which the author forces the reader to glimpse by breaking down his habitual and superficial perceptions. The transference also tends to enlarge the characters: by remaining permanent in the midst of changes, they become mythical beings, transcending their avatars. It is worth noticing that the word "avatar"[4] is used in two of the above quotations and in the description of Joanna's sexual frenzy, and that Percy Grimm, one of the avatars of Fate as far as Joe is concerned, provokes the image of Vishnu, the god with nine avatars, in his Juggernaut (p. 435).

THE APPEARANCE OF THE CHARACTERS

The enlargement of the characters is seen again in Faulkner's typical manner of introducing them, or rather of not introducing them, for very often they seem to materialize suddenly out of thin air or to have been there already, before one's awareness of them. In this way they assume superhuman proportions. The appearance in Jefferson of Thomas Sutpen in Miss Rosa's outraged account, or in Mr. Compson's soberer one, is an unforgettable example.[5] Every time we see him, Christmas seems to be already there, possessing other people in his glance even before they know that he is there. After he has knocked down McEachern, Joe receives the same impression of Mame: "He saw her for the first time, without surprise, having apparently materialised out of thin air, motionless, with that diamondsurfaced tranquillity . . ." (p. 204). Often Faulkner describes objects in the same way. The train which passes Doane's Mill has the effect of an apparition issuing from the hills, "wailing like a banshee" (p. 3). In view of this, even the wagon creaking toward Lena can be seen as an instance of the same technique: "The wagon mounts the hill toward her. She passed it about a mile back down the road. It was standing beside the road . . ." (p. 5). As in the first sight of Lena at the beginning of the chapter, Faulkner imposes the image so suddenly that it is afterwards ineradicable, in the same way as an object glimpsed in a sudden *flash* imprints itself upon the eye, and the image is then embroidered and enriched in a *flashback*. Thus, objects and characters appear immobile, their motion being less important than their presence, because the reader suddenly perceives their presence with something of a shock, as he has not seen them appear. The impression that they have always been there adds to their actual temporal dimension, making them akin to immemorial myths.

CHARACTERS AND MYTHS

Even in his early works Faulkner made use of biblical parallels, particularly the story of Christ, and of allusions to ancient myths, with which he was well acquainted, especially after he had read the abridged version of *The Golden Bough* (published in 1922) in New Orleans in 1925.[6] However, although in a complex novel like *A Fable* the mythical analogue is a vital part of the structure, in *Light in August* the parallels are neither sufficiently sustained nor consistent with one another for this to be so. They are mainly used for the enlargement of the characters.

As has often been remarked the characters' names are full of suggestions. As Byron thinks, "a man's name, which is supposed to be just the sound for who he is, can be somehow an augur of what he will do, if other men can only read the meaning in time" (p. 29). The last page of *Sartoris* suggests that the family's whole history was implicit in the sound of its name. Replying to a question on the significance of the names in *Light in August*, Faulkner said:

> That is out of the tradition of the pre-Elizabethans, who named their characters according to what they looked like or what they did. . . . Of course, it seems to me that those people named themselves, but I can see where that came from—it came from . . . my memory of the old miracle plays, the morality plays in early English literature. Chaucer.[7]

It is dangerous to pursue these parallels too far, however. There is a risk of falling into absurdity, as did Beekman W. Cottrell, who saw Joanna Burden as John the Baptist because they have the same initials, and was determined that Hightower should be Pontius Pilate: with great ingenuity he discovered that the Latin word "pons" could mean the floor of a tower.[8] At most a character's name may suggest one facet of his personality, but such indications are never carried through in systematic mythical references. "Burden" may evoke the load of fanatical Calvinism and dead tradition under which Joanna labors, and "Byron" could be an ironic parallel with the Romantic poet of that name, who was surely happier in his conquests. "Lena," a diminutive of Helen, suggests the archetypal woman, and "Grove" nature, the living earth. Hightower lives, it is true, cut off from his fellows as in a tower. Finally, as has been enthusiastically pointed out by many critics, Joe Christmas and Jesus Christ have the same initials.

Certain analogies or images do have the effect of raising the character's stature, as already noted in the instance of Joanna Burden. The elliptical reference to Medusa takes her beyond her nymphomania to archetypal sexuality, hence evil: her "wild hair, each strand of which would seem to come alive like octopus tentacles" (p. 245), suggests Medusa's phallic serpents. But Faulkner is never a slave to mythology, rather he interprets it according to his own ends. In the instance mentioned above, as Joe feels himself "sucked down into a bottomless morass" (p. 246), Faulkner finds the image of the octopus more apt than that of snakes. Later, though, Joanna's menacing pistol is compared to the vicious, "arched head of a snake" (p. 267), and Joanna, like Medusa, is beheaded. Likewise there is a glancing evocation of Vishnu in his Juggernaut in Percy Grimm's relentless pursuit of Joe, and McEachern's pursuit in the same temporary role as God's avenging agent inspires Faulkner to coin the word "juggernautish" (p. 190). Oriental mythology is probably Hightower's backdrop, as he is twice compared to an eastern idol (pp. 83 and 298), like Marlow in *Heart of Darkness*. The image of the wheel could symbolize either the Wheel of Law which Bhudda saw spinning before him in his vision, or the wheels of Vishnu's chariot being dragged through the sand by his disciples.

All these references, but particularly the last ones, are too brief to allow of definitive interpretation.[9] Their effectiveness is in contributing, however fleetingly, to the significances gathering around a character to increase his stature. However, in two cases, the mythical references are relatively persistent and coherent. The analogies between Joe Christmas and Christ are obvious: Joe was found on the doorstep of an orphanage one Christmas night, and on his arrival at the McEacherns' his foster mother washed his feet. There is a consistent analogy between his last few days and the Holy Week: he is betrayed for money by his disciple, Brown; on the Tuesday, he turns Negro worshippers out of their church; on the Thursday, he eats in a Negro cabin and for the first time thinks of the blacks as his brothers; on the Friday, he gives himself up to the justice of men. When he is asked if he is indeed called Christmas, he does not deny it; he is struck in the face by Halliday and suffers uncomplainingly, while Hines incites the crowd to lynch him. During his confinement in Mottstown prison, the guards recruited by Grimm play poker all the time. The ripping of his clothes by Grimm's knife is perhaps brutally reminiscent of the sharing out of Christ's garments. Hightower continually thinks of Christmas's death as a crucifixion (pp. 347–48); and finally, his spurting blood evokes in the spectators' minds an ascensionlike image. [10]

This is not necessarily proof that Christmas should be seen as a Christ figure, as has too often been assumed. In the first place, only the human side of Christ is suggested, the suffering Christ of Isaiah chapter 53, "He is despised and rejected of men. . . . He was oppressed, and he was afflicted, yet he opened not his mouth"; the victorious Christ of the New Testament is ignored. Moreover, Christmas is an ironic inversion of Christ, as his life is one of hatred and violence towards men. Although he finally accepts the Negroes as his brothers and eats their food, they reject him and fear him, as do most of the people he meets during his last week. Less obviously, he has ironically been corrupted by Joanna and McEachern, both of whom he strangely resembles as he perpetuates the same intolerance against which he rebels. Ultimately, he destroys himself: his crucifixion, far from being a supreme sacrifice of the self, is the crucifixion of himself. His death is almost as much a suicide as Popeye's in *Sanctuary.*

Through constant association with the earth, Lena, too, rises above the limitations of her actual life. She is part of "the old earth of and with and by which she lives" (p. 23). She has its fertility, and Hightower knows that her pregnancy, and all others to come, are manifestations of the endless regeneration of the earth she so calmly obeys (p. 384). She seems to be "hearing and feeling the implacable and immemorial earth" (p. 26), and she sways to its eternal rhythms: in her absence of haste and perturbation, she partakes of the "untroubled unhaste of a change of season" (p. 47) or of the August afternoon, hanging hypnotized by its own heat and balmy silence, on which we first see her, "swollen, slow, deliberate, unhurried, and tireless as augmenting afternoon itself" (p. 7). She has plenty of time, as she tells Byron: "A few minutes wouldn't make no difference" (p. 47); and she knows that everything will come at its appointed hour: "I reckon a family ought to all be together when a chap comes. Specially the first one. I reckon the Lord will see to that" (p. 18; cf. p. 285).

The association of Woman with immemorial earth is an idea dear to Faulkner. It already appears in one of his early stories, "Out of Nazareth" (1925), in the description of a boy who seems to be part of the earth in his serene beauty: "He reminded one of a pregnant woman in his calm belief that nature, the earth which had spawned him, would care for him, that he was serving his appointed ends, had served his appointed end and now need only wait."[11] This could well be the sketched outline of Lena Grove, Eula Varner, Dewey Dell, Laverne Shumann, of the placid, bovine Jenny in *Mosquitoes,* of the anonymous woman in "Old Man," and even of the engaged Judith Sutpen, living in an enclosed, serene, and timeless world of her own. Thus, Lena grows into some sort of earth goddess, the Mother Earth of all ancient mythologies. Faulkner clearly saw her as the August light, which pervades the whole work and gives it its title. She is associated with the first civilizations which shed their serene light on newborn humanity:

> In August in Mississippi there's a few days somewhere about the middle of the month when suddenly there's a foretaste of fall, it's cool, there's a lambence, a luminous quality to the light, as though it came not from just today but from back in the old classic times. It might have fauns and satyrs and the gods and—from Greece, from Olympus in it somewhere. It lasts just for a day or two, then it's gone, but every year in August that occurs in my country, and that's all that title meant, it was just to me a pleasant evocative title because it reminded me of that time, of a luminosity older than our Christian civilization. Maybe the connection was with Lena Grove, who had something of that pagan quality of being able to assume everything . . . . And that was all that meant, just that luminous lambent quality of an older light than ours.[12]

Lena is therefore a complete and rounded being, timeless, and so it is fitting that the first chapter and indeed the whole book should be in circular form. The double evocation of circularity and eternity is pinpointed in the image of the urn, applied to Lena on page 5. Almost inevitably, this image conjures up the urn of Keats, for whom Faulkner expressed an early admiration, which remained unchanged ever afterwards.[13] The urn is Lena herself:[14] her name does in fact echo the lines in Keat's poem:

> What leaf-fring'd legend haunts about thy shape
> Of deities or mortals, or of both.

The apostrophes to the urn could as accurately be addressed to Lena:

> Thou still unravished bride of quietness,
> Thou foster-child of silence and slow time . . .
> Thou, silent form, dost tease us out of thought
> As does eternity: Cold Pastoral!

However, Faulkner does not restrict himself to the Mother Goddess frame of reference. With her faded blue clothes and palm leaf fan, details heavily insisted upon in the first chapter, Lena also suggests the Virgin Mary. Thus she is simultaneously Helen, because of her name, a Mother Goddess, and the Virgin. Faulkner's technique cannot, in view of this, be construed as the strict establishment of parallels between characters and myths. Lena is obviously a syncretic combination of feminine myths. Similarly, Christmas is fleetingly seen as Faustus, with just a hint of sulphurous fumes (p. 194). So it is unwise to seek a definite analogy between Joe and Christ because of the risk of deforming or fixing, and so limiting, the potential significance of the character. Such a procedure invites the twisting of facts to suit a hypothesis anyway: even Holman, in an otherwise excellent article, is guilty. He makes Christmas die at the age of thirty-three, and he is not alone in this distortion, although it is plainly stated that Christmas was thirty-three when he arrived in Jefferson and that his affair with Joanna lasted for three years.

It must be remembered then that the use of mythological allusion is only one of the many tools, as Faulkner himself might have said, used to extend a character beyond the limitations of his actual context. It helps to surround the character with an aura of suggested significance which can, allowing for perception and knowledge on the part of the reader, raise him to immemorial dimensions. The Christian legend is one of many in this sense, the one which Faulkner happened to know best, as he explained at the University of Virginia:

> Remember, the writer must write out of his background. He must write out of what he knows and the Christian legend is part of any Christian's background, especially the background of a country boy, a Southern country boy. My life was passed, my childhood, in a very small Mississippi town, and that was

part of my background. . . . It has nothing to do with how much of it I might believe or disbelieve—it's just there.

That's a matter of reaching into the lumber room to get out something which seems to the writer the most effective way to tell what he is trying to tell. . . . Everyone that has had the story of Christ and the Passion as a part of his Christian background will in time draw from that. There was no deliberate intent to repeat it. That the people to me come first. The symbolism comes second. [15]

THE AMBIGUITY OF THE CHARACTERS

In contrast to *Absalom, Absalom!,* the ambiguity of the characters does not arise from the multiplicity of points of view. In *Light in August* the narrators are far less important and are not used to create a kaleidoscopic series of irreconcilable images of the same character. The various narrations add diversity to the tone of the novel and make it more alive and direct. And Byron Bunch is essentially the indispensable coordinator of the different focal points. Thus the narrators serve the overall structure rather than the drawing of the characters. Faulkner does nevertheless present widely divergent views of some characters. For instance, Christmas is at first known only through rumor, which paints him as grim, malevolent, a fatal person with snakelike attributes. However, from chapter 6 onwards, as the reader reconstructs his past and lives with him through the warping and wounding experiences, he takes on a totally different appearance, and arouses the reader's sympathy in spite of his acts. Yet the first impression is never effaced: it is simply that the two aspects are merged, with neither one dimming or obliterating the other.

In this novel the ambiguity does not often arise from the narrative technique, but is rather inherent in the significance the author wishes to confer upon his characters, as has been seen in relation to the mythical connotations.

Lena, for example, has faith in nature and in people's generosity, but she also calculates upon both, as Mrs. Armstid clearly feels. She smiles, but she is none the less implacable in the pursuit of her aim. Surprisingly, she resembles Anse Bundren, the father in *As I lay Dying,* in several ways. Moreover, she is at the same time rich in her innate certitude and almost subhumanly empty. The innocence and depth of her look (p. 5) are not symptomatic of one and the same quality, but of two opposed facets of her personality. The first two adjectives applied to her, "unshakeable" and "sheeplike" (p. 4), already indicate the contradiction expressed in her face later on: "her grave face which had either nothing in it, or everything, all knowledge" (p. 409); this reminds one of Anse Bundren, in whom there "lurks a wisdom too profound or too inert for even thought."[16] Lena may evoke a fertility goddess, but she is also the stolid bovine, or "sheeplike," peasant woman. Her serenity is, in the last analysis, that of animals as extolled in Whitman's "Song of Myself" (section 32):

> I think I could turn and live with animals, they are so placid and self-contain'd, . . .
> They do not sweat and whine about their condition,
> They do not lie awake in the dark and weep for their sins, . . .
> Not one is dissatisfied, not one is demented with the mania of owning things. . . .

The immemorial qualities of endurance and of permanence which she represents are inseparable from intellectual limitation. Her last words, the last of the book, are aesthetically pleasing, but they are also comic, for they emphasize her automatic persistence in her aim, and her total imperviousness to the tragedies going on around her. Unlike Hightower, she is unchanged at the end of the novel. As Bergson has shown, this mechanical aspect of human behavior is a basic source of comedy.

Hightower also is an ambiguous character. In the last paragraph of chapter 20, the return of the vision is disturbing and forbids any absolute certainty that his confession has really brought about his redemption. In his case, however, it may be more a matter of uncertainty than of ambiguity, and for two reasons. Faulkner has not wholly succeeded in portraying, from the interior, Hightower's obsession with his grandfather. In spite of its brilliance, chapter 20 does not make the fixation plausible. Compared to the treatment given to Christmas, Hightower's childhood experiences appear vague and abstract, recapitulated rather than relived. Faulkner was probably wrong to caricature him in fact: in the scenes with Byron, he is too much like one of Sherwood Anderson's grotesques to be then turned into the moral center of the novel. He is not quite coherent enough to bear the weight imposed on him by the structure of the book. The second reason for his lack of conviction as a character is that he develops during the novel. Faulkner appears to be less able to show a character's evolution than to reveal gradually a character already complete in his imagination, and who only appears to grow because the reader gains deeper knowledge of him as time goes on. Most of Faulkner's characters are of the past and are only seen in the present at the height of their development.

Joe Christmas, as has been seen, is both a Christ figure and an inversion, or perversion, of Christ. His death, too, cannot be clearly interpreted. Is the peace he finds at this time the acceptance of himself and of others, or is it only the result of extreme physical and mental fatigue: *"I am tired of running of having to carry my life like it was a basket of eggs"* (p. 319)? The only solution his own inarticulate mind produces could not be called an explanation, unless by an ultimate stroke of irony it were the only one: "suddenly the true answer comes to him. He feels dry and light. 'I don't have to bother about having to eat anymore,' he thinks. 'That's what it is'" (p. 320). His death is described from the outside with no hint of his thoughts. Is it, like Christ's death, a supreme identification with humanity, or is it a more or less conscious suicide? Is his castration a symbolic crucifixion or merely a demonstration of Grimm's sadism? The significance of his symbolic ascension is also clouded, especially as the chapter ends on the unbelievable scream of the siren. As an ascension it is travesty; as an apotheosis it is a cruel parody.

The questions remain unanswerable, or open to many answers. As a result, the characters have no single, unequivocal interpretation. Because of their ambiguity they cannot be overidentified with any one myth or archetype, or become allegorical like some of Hawthorne's characters. They remain somehow undefined, complex, and contradictory, impossible to categorize or finally to judge. Thus Faulkner forces the reader to suspend his faculty of judgment and simply share their feelings and experiences rather than analyze them intellectually. With the possible exception of Hightower, a character's ambiguity adds to his actuality in the reader's imagination. Because of this, and mostly because of a highly personal technique in drawing characters, some of those in *Light in August* are among Faulkner's greatest successes.

4

The Landscape[1]

IN *LIGHT IN AUGUST* there are few long descriptions of landscape or setting. Faulkner does not break the flow of his narrative with minute descriptive details of scenery or dwelling, of sounds or colors or shadow effects. The descriptions, usually brief, are either in the form of quickly sketched outlines which situate an event, characterizing it for future reference, and which allow of a respite without causing an interruption (e.g., in chapter 4), or they are glimpses of a landscape seen through a character's perceptions or related to his acts, so that Faulkner's scenery always appears to be somehow inhabited. For instance, the road is unimportant except as it is seen in relation to Lena as she gazes at it; the street is equally so without the imprisoned Christmas; the Burden house likewise without the old maid or the memory of her presence. It is thus not surprising that the landscape should bear a strange resemblance to the characters inhabiting it, and have the same quality of unreality and haunting actuality.

IMMOBILITY

The landscape is in fact largely defined in terms of light and shade, and of stillness and movement. The first impression is that the immobility of the landscape is of a different nature than that furious and violent immobility of the characters. Just as the monotonous humming of the myriads of insects which forms a ceaseless sonorous background to Jefferson[2] and is a gauge of the silence or of the other sounds seems an aural metaphor for eternity, so the landscape seems to be a visual one. The unchanging street remains a constant prison for Christmas, the road Lena follows is a monotonous, unvarying repetition of itself. Armstid's wagon, an avatar of the wagons Lena has traveled in for a month, appears to hang motionless in space. The reference to Keats's "Ode" is thus perfectly appropriate, for the silent form of the urn on whose flank Lena moves "forever and without progress" (p. 5) is also a symbol of eternity. On this August afternoon, the landscape and all that Lena sees seem to be, like her, suspended outside time, as though, with the absence of movement, time or timelessness were merged with space and took on all its attributes. The monotonous succession of days and nights is no longer a measure of time passing, for it is "already measured thread being rewound onto a spool" (p. 6).[3]

Such a suspension does not however infer absolute motionlessness. The landscape in *Light in August* is never immutable or dead: it retains potential movement as do the momentarily stilled characters. In fact, as in a dream or nightmare, the landscape is slowly altered, and the shadows quiver and swell monstrously; or it can appear to glide past the characters, while they remain apparently stationary. The most striking example of this deceptive immobility is in the description of what Doane's Mill will look like after it has been abandoned (p. 2). The words do not suggest a dead or inhuman scene. On the contrary, the ghostly derelict equipment takes on the human properties of wonderment or outrage, felt by those who left it behind, or by those who will come silently to gaze upon it. The adjectives are more applicable to people than to objects: "staring," "stubborn," "baffled," "bemused." The negatives continually suggest the presence of what they deny ("motionless," "unsmoking," "unplowed," "untilled"), translating the former life and movement below the apparent death and stillness. Finally, certain verbs used as present participles suggest both movement and permanence, and evoke the slow, unceasing transformation of the landscape: "rising," "lifting," "gutting slowly." It is so unreal and fantastic that it could not be reproduced or photographed. Yet it is unforgettably actual: it is the expression of an inner, imaginary landscape.

COLORS

Light, or its absence, is even more important than immobility in defining the landscape of *Light in August.* Hence the relative rarity of color touches only makes their effect more striking. They do not describe an actual scene so much as they express a personal vision. Yellow is the color of sunrise ("the gray and yellow of dawn," p. 102) before the harsh, implacable glare of noon has obliterated every nuance of color. There is often a hint of preciosity in Faulkner's descriptions of the tints of dawn: the rising sun may be "primrose" (pp. 102, 375) or "jonquilcolored" (p. 314): Faulkner's apparent predilection for this color leads him to use it again and again, for instance, in *The Wild Palms* and *The Hamlet.* As daylight fades, the yellow returns with ominous undertones: it turns copper, as on the evening when Addie Bundren "lays dying," or when Hightower makes his confession: "that fading copper light would seem almost audible, like a dying yellow fall of trumpets . . ." (p. 441).[4] At dusk, the light takes on a purple hue and is again expressed through studiedly refined floral equivalents (perhaps a trace of Faulkner's acquaintance with symbolist and "decadent" poetry): "Then the copper faded into lilac, into the fading lilac of full dusk" (p. 223). Later on, in the fantastic stillness of dusk, before everything is submerged in darkness, the light is a glaucous green shade: "the world hangs in a green suspension in color and texture like light through colored glass" (p. 443).

These examples show that the rare and studied colors of Faulkner's world are designed less to describe a given landscape than to render impressions and feelings. Copper is the color of the other world evoked by the dying light of day. Purple is tragic, and appropriately the color of Mrs. Hines's gown, less in description than in suggestion of her tragic being; so much so that Faulkner eventually uses "regal and moribund" (p. 420) instead of purple, substituting the connotations of the color for the color itself, creating it anew from within.

SHADES OF LIGHT

The landscape is less remarkable for its colors than for the striking use of black and white, light and shadow. The modifier "pale" recurs frequently: Faulkner often uses it as a color in itself. The eyes of several characters are pale (this is even more noticeable in *As I Lay Dying*), bleached like the landscape which only exists by and for its inhabitants, an extension of their gaze.

The incandescent light of the South obliterates not only colors but also, strangely, shadows. The landscape then appears unreal, has no depth or distance: it becomes impossible to position objects, which hang in dimensionless space, hypnotized by the unremitting glare: "Though the mules plod in a steady and unflagging hypnosis, the vehicle does not seem to progress. It seems to hang suspended in the middle distance forever and forever . . ." (p. 5); "Fields and woods seem to hang in some inescapable middle distance, at once static and fluid, quick, like mirages" (pp. 24–25). Such are the characteristics of this landscape: at once static and fluid, it has no fixed dimension or cohesion. Even sounds have no source by which one could re-create a three-dimensional space or orientate it, witness the sound of Armstid's wagon: "as though out of some trivial and unimportant region beyond even distance, the sound of it seems to come slow and terrific and without meaning, as though it were a ghost travelling a half mile ahead of its own shape" (p. 6). Again and again, Faulkner insists on the oneiric quality of the landscape ("hypnosis," "ghost," "dreamlike," "somnolence"), and the rhythm of the prose contributes to the hypnotic effect, with balanced repetitions and regularly alternating stressed and unstressed syllables turning prose into poetry: "as sight and sense drowsily merge and blend" (p. 6; at the manuscript stage, Faulkner had not yet achieved this deliberate effect: "as sight and sense become one"). The sense of unreality is increased by an abundant use of oxymorons, linking mutually exclusive ideas: "moving without progress," "slow and terrific," "dry sluggish reports" (pp. 5, 25). This landscape is unreal and impossible, but as actual and as inevitable as the closed world of dreams, where, isolated from outside comparison with reality, the landscape becomes perfectly coherent and real.

As the harsh glare fades and fails, shadows and shades of light reappear, re-creating the illusion of relief, or coherence. The landscape is then expressed in black and white, pale and dark. It is only to be expected that the striking image of the photograph should recur as often as it does: "He watched his body grow white out of the darkness like a kodak print emerging from the liquid" (p. 100); the film negative, reversing light and dark, is also frequently used (instances may be found in *Sanctuary, The Wild Palms, Intruder in the Dust,* and "Victory"). People and objects now take on a different relationship to their background, hence the use of such phrases and prepositions as "in silhouette," "upon," and, particularly, "against" and "out of." It seems that Faulkner distinguishes between his settings by the varying degrees of darkness of their planes or surfaces. He juggles with shadows, and even lays shadow on shadow: "the bitten shadows of the unwinded maples

seem to toss faintly upon the August darkness" (p. 70);
"the cabins were shaped blackly out of blackness by the
faint, sultry glow of kerosene lamps" (p. 107). Twilight
fascinates him, which explains the rich vocabulary associated
with this final and fragile suspension of light. *Light in
August, As I Lay Dying,* and *Sanctuary* provide striking
examples of this vocabulary: "to fade," "to fail," "faint,"
"defunctive," etc. He is equally fascinated by moonlit nights,
when the scenery is colorless, "moonblanched" (p. 198).
At such times the shadows seem to come alive with movement, and the vocabulary suggests trembling, nascent, or
fantastically disintegrating forms: "bitten shadows," "to toss"
(p. 70), "to bulge" (p. 108), "to loom," "to drift" (p. 109),
"to float," "to dissolve," "to fade" (p. 110), "tremulous"
(pp. 107, 108). *Sanctuary* is equally rich in similar examples.
The setting eventually assumes aspects of the characters
living in it and even becomes an extension or projection
of their essential being. This is true of the streets where
Christmas is lost, a shadow among shadows: "In the wide,
empty, shadowbrooded street he looked like a phantom,
a spirit, strayed out of its own world, and lost" (p. 106).
In the moonlight, McEachern's house, which Joe is on the
point of leaving forever, strikes him as having taken on
some of the characteristics of the foster parents who threaten
his integrity: "The house squatted in the moonlight, dark,
profound, a little treacherous. It was as though in the
moonlight the house had acquired personality: threatful,
deceptive" (p. 160).

The depth of this apparently layered setting is illusory.
One plane is visible only because it is silhouetted against
another. Although they may be perceived together, their
ceaseless shifting and changing allows no coherent form,
no third dimension. Faulkner's landscape is as physically
"depthless" as his characters. In the blaze of noon, the
landscape dissolves in too much light, yet remains actual
and visible; in the evening, the several planes reappear, but

separately, not forming a solid world. As much as his characters, Faulkner's landscapes remain in suspension.

INNER LANDSCAPE

It becomes more and more evident that the landscape is an inner one, connected with the characters or described through them, a projection or a reflection of them. Significantly, Faulkner sometimes uses the same words for his characters as for their setting: "stubborn" describes both the derelict sawmill and McKinley, who works there (pp. 2 and 4), "unflagging" applies to Lena and to the mules (pp. 4 and 5), "deliberate" is equally apt for the wagons in which Lena travels and for her own appearance (pp. 5, 7, 9, 12), and when Christmas, panic-stricken, tries to escape from Freedman Town, "glaring" or "glare" is the key word of the passage, and is used indiscriminately of Joe's looks, his teeth, his lips, of the women's arms in the darkness, and of the lights from the town (pp. 107–108). In the same way, the sawmill reflects and shares the astonishment of the men, and Hightower's garden, with its constricted lawn, "lowgrowing maples," and "bushing crape myrtle and syringa," which seem to choke and hide the house (p. 52), is the perfect image of the minister's cramped and useless life. When Joe has left Freedman Town, he passes "a horizontal and cylindrical tank like the torso of a beheaded mastodon" (p. 108), the monstrous replica of an image he already carries within himself, and which will become real a few hours later. On the Friday morning of his surrender Joe inhales the dawn, "feeling with each breath himself diffuse in the neutral grayness": he is filled with the peace of daybreak itself and of the "tentative waking of birds" (p. 313).

Just as the characters are the incarnation of the author's impressions and feelings rather than realistic creations, so the landscape is the expression of an inner vision, none the less real for being abstract. Faulkner uses many comparisons and metaphors, subjective equivalents of his vision, in the descriptions of landscape and characters alike. In *As I Lay Dying* Peabody considers the predicament of man formed by the land which bore him: "That's the one trouble with this country: everything, weather, all, hangs on too long. Like our rivers, our land: opaque, slow, violent; shaping and creating the life of man in its implacable and brooding image" (pp. 43–44). However, this only shows one side of the equation of what is in effect an interaction. Since the landscape only exists for and through a character's being, it takes on a symbolic value and becomes the imaginary accompaniment to the action. Its light or darkness really belongs to the characters, and it takes on the color, feel, and smell of their obsessions. The air Christmas breathes in Freedman Town, the night which enfolds him, touches him, smothers him—these are the very breath and "fecund-mellow" voices of the Negroes, the emanation of the womb the black quarter represents for him: a moment later, "the cold hard air" symbolizes the white quarter and masculinity regained (p. 107). At the tender age of fourteen he already attributed a particular odor to the evening star, "rich and heavy as a jasmine bloom" (p. 148). This is Venus, the symbol of Woman, which he, alone among his comrades, resisted, and which has for him this oversweet, pervasive jasmine scent. In the same way, Quentin Compson and Horace Benbow connect femininity with the sickly smell of honeysuckle. Thus Faulkner uses all the senses to render the impression given by the landscape. Visual sensations predominate, but the senses of hearing and smell are not neglected, and they often combine in striking instances of synesthesia: the evening star has a perfume, twilight becomes a sound, the clump of willows, invisible in the darkness, is felt and heard. As a result, such an unreal landscape is strangely actual and obsessive, particularly as the reader's perceptions of it are the same as the character's. A Faulknerian landscape is above all the image of a state of mind.

5

The Themes

Light in August is a complex novel with many themes: the racial problem, the search for identity, the alienation and isolation of man, the burden of Calvinism, fate, sexuality, the rejection of life, or alternatively, the humble acceptance of it. The themes are not debated in the abstract, but appear in the course of the action. It is thus essential to examine them in relation to the characters in whom they are exposed (and who are no longer to be studied from a technical point of view) and to the structure of the novel. In fact, the thematic analysis of *Light in August* could be summed up in the fundamental opposition on which the whole book is based: the contrast between Christmas and Joanna on the one hand, and Lena and Byron on the other, the two antithetical couples. As racial and sexual problems are at the root of Christmas's alienation, as his search for identity appears to be in both racial and sexual terms, and as he is a central figure, these two themes should be examined first.

RACE

Unlike *Intruder in the Dust,* race is not the central theme of *Light in August.* The subject of the former is the coexistence of the races in the South, and it takes the form of an examination and condemnation of the anonymous, irrational reactions of the white community. Faced with the defiance of a Negro, the community can but react according to a fixed code. Chick Mallinson's attempt to break away from the code is a true initiation of the boy into manhood. The racial problem is present in *Light in August,* but it has sometimes been clouded by misunderstanding. Although Christmas never really knows whether he has Negro blood, as soon as Brown states that he has, nobody in Jefferson doubts it, not even Hightower at first. Once they believe it, he becomes a Negro in their eyes, and they treat him as such. The community needs a scapegoat, and that this should be a Negro is reassuring: the ritual punishment purges the white community after the threat to its integrity, and confirms the code for and by which it lives. To doubt the justice of the code would be to doubt the identity of the community, as Hightower appreciates: "'Since to pity him would be to admit selfdoubt and to hope for and need pity themselves. They will do it gladly, gladly. That's why it is so terrible, terrible, terrible'" (p. 348).

In his book *Anti-Semite and Jew,* Sartre makes a brilliant analysis of the workings of the anti-Semitic mind, or passion, rather. He shows that the anti-Semite actually needs the Jew as a means of camouflaging his own mediocrity and self-fear, by establishing his superiority over a being who is by definition bad: he thus provides himself with a personality at very little cost. He then recovers a feeling of equality, even in the heart of a strongly hierarchical society, which stems directly from his very participation in the anti-Semitic community. However, as Sartre so rightly says, "the equalitarian society that the anti-Semite believes in is like that of mobs or those instantaneous societies which come into being at a lynching or during a scandal. Equality in them is the product of the non-differentiation of functions. The social bond is anger. . . . Thus the person is drowned in the crowd, and the ways of thinking and reacting of the group are of a purely primitive type."[1] For anti-Semitism presupposes a Manichean concept of society, and so a naively optimistic belief that harmony will follow naturally once the evil (that is, the Jew) is eliminated or the stain cleansed. This is obviously an attitude at once lazy and reassuring, which allows one to indulge, with a clear conscience, in violence and the fascination of evil. Thus, the anti-Semite easily becomes "a sadist with a pure heart".[2] The reactions of the Jefferson community to the news that Christmas has Negro blood (and the people ask nothing better than to believe this simple and satisfying explanation), and equally the *passion* which takes hold of Percy Grimm, becoming his sole raison d'être and justifying him totally even in murder, are both easily recognizable within the terms of Sartre's analysis.

However, Faulkner leaves Joe's origins in doubt so that the racial problem becomes an internal one, and it is this doubt which plunges Joe into his violent search for identity and into isolation. His tragic destiny is a perfect illustration of the disastrous effects of racism in a man's consciousness, for in fact, he is black only in his own mind, and he believes it only because it is what others believe of him. This is precisely what one of Faulkner's most lucid (even if sick) characters, Quentin Compson, has come to understand while living in the North: "a nigger is not a person so much as a form of behaviour; a sort of obverse reflection of the white people he lives among."[3] In showing how the anguish torturing Joe Christmas is above all the poisoning of his consciousness caused by the idea other people have of him, Faulkner exposes the essence of racism more radically than in *Intruder in the Dust*, and with no trace of sentimentality or idealism. He demonstrates that the biological traits are secondary, literally superficial, agreeing in this with Sartre's conclusions.[4]

For other characters, black blood has moral even more

than biological significance. They see it as a stain on the soul, as a sign of evil and of God's wrath, as in "Benito Cereno." Thus for Joanna's grandfather, Negroes and the Southern slaveowners are similarly branded: "Damn, lowbuilt black folks: lowbuilt because of the weight of the wrath of God, black because of the sin of human bondage staining their blood and flesh. . . . But we done freed them now, both black and white alike. They'll bleach out now. In a hundred years they will be white folks again" (p. 234). The succeeding generations of the Burden family see the two races doomed to be a curse for each other. In Joanna's tortured mind, distorted by a fanatical Calvinism which becomes a morbid obsession, the Negro race is a black shadow engulfing and smothering the rest of the world, a perverted image of Original Sin which no Crucifixion can ever redeem:

> I seemed to see the black shadow in the shape of a cross. And it seemed like the white babies were struggling, even before they drew breath, to escape from the shadow that was not only upon them but beneath them too, flung out like their arms were flung out, as if they were nailed to the cross. (p. 239)

A Negro signifies different things to different characters, for he is basically a mirror which reflects back the prejudices and obsessions of all who look into it. These prejudices seem at last to be acknowledged for what they are by the spectators of Joe's death, who are never to lose the memory of the "peaceful and unfathomable and unbearable eyes" of the dying man: Christmas dies, but the shame lives on.

FEMININITY AND SEXUALITY

Christmas becomes an outcast not only because of the image of himself reflected back to him by society, but also because of his rejection of feminity and sexuality. This theme is followed almost exclusively in Joe's experiences.

The shape of his whole life is molded by women. His mother, because she lay with a man believed black, is responsible for his alienation and for his violent and vain attempts to find an identity. He is sent away from the orphanage because he is the unwitting and uncomprehending witness to the sexual relations of the dietitian and the interne. Mrs. McEachern's blundering solicitude confirms him in his refusal of all feminine tenderness. Bobbie Allen's seeming betrayal triggers his fifteen-year-long flight. Finally, Joanna Burden corrupts and destroys him by her sexual frenzy.

Christmas must flee women or kill them to ensure his physical security, and even more to protect his integrity: here as in *Sanctuary*, they often symbolize irregularity and illegality. His life is indeed a succession of temptations from women: if he surrenders, he compromises his integrity and upsets his conception of the world. At the orphanage his world was defined in terms of reward and punishment, good and evil. In withholding punishment the dietitian confused this order and destroyed its logic. Before this he had experienced maternal tenderness, offered him by the child Alice. The episode with the dietitian precluded any recurrence of such feeling, except when he loved Bobbie, later, at the age of eighteen. However, Joe's desire for purity and his idealism are both destroyed when Bobbie's indisposition reawakens the horror he thought dead, and when she betrays him, as he sees it. Once more he repudiates the world of femininity, which threatens the world of masculinity and arouses in him a physical revulsion, latent ever since he vomited behind a curtain as he crouched among woman's clothes. At the McEacherns' he expects and accepts the blows which reestablish the balance between good and evil: but he refuses the merciful intercession of money and secretly offered food. These compensations threaten to upset the strict laws of the world in which he lives, where love and compassion are snares and dangers.

While rejecting Calvinism as a religion, he does retain its modes of thought.

Joe's antipathy for femininity is seen in his horror of sexuality. To analyze his obsessions one must look once more at his descent into Freedman Town, which is a crisis in his life: it at once precedes and provokes the murder which causes his own death. More important, it is a symbol for his entire life in that it contains and crystallizes into a single moment all the fears and hatreds which have alienated him from humanity and determined his destiny. In this scene, his dual conception of the world is made clear for the first time: male against female, dry and cold against moist and warm, White against Black, good against evil. For him the distinctions are clear-cut, and confusion is insupportable.

For Joe, as for his grandfather, Man and White are of God, while Woman and Black are of the Devil. The Negro world and the female world are both moist and dark, overpowering, clinging, smothering. They are classed together in his mind ever since his days at the orphanage: the dietitian's venomous cry, "You little nigger bastard"(p. 114), is associated with his first contact with sexuality (the incident with the dietitian and the interne), which he cannot forget even though he did not understand it at the time ("Memory believes before knowing remembers"). At age fourteen, when he enters the barn where the Negro girl awaits him, his two fears are combined, as they are in the striking word "womanshenegro," and he experiences that same dizziness as he stands trembling on the edge of the abyss that he feels later in his life with Joanna, and again in Freedman Town. There, lost in the shadowy depths of the Negro quarter, a symbol of the abyss which has threatened him since his birth, his masculinity is nullified: "It was as though he and all other manshaped life about him had been returned to the lightless hot wet primogenitive Female" (p. 107).

It is interesting to note that in *The Wild Palms,* Harry Wilbourne, in his first sexual encounter at the age of twenty-seven, feels the same terror as Joe Christmas, but Wilbourne's is intensified because of the many years during which he has repudiated his self and resigned himself to never tasting "the passionate tragic ephemeral loves of adolescence"; he has reached a state of mind where he cannot move beyond the memory of the instant of his fall over "the dark precipice," at which moment his life seemed to end:

> You remember: the precipice, the dark precipice; all mankind before you went over it and lived and all after you will but that means nothing to you because they can't tell you, forewarn you, what to do in order to survive . . . the darkness, the falling, the thunder of solitude, the shock, the death, the moment when, stopped physically by the ponderable clay, you yet feel all your life rush out of you into the pervading immemorial blind receptive matrix, the hot fluid blind foundation—grave-womb or womb-grave, it's all one. [5]

The terror, the plunge into the abyss, the negation of masculinity in primordial femininity, and the fascination for death, here exaggerated by an introverted and surely masochistic mentality, are the same as are seen in the far more simpleminded Christmas, and they are also depicted by remarkably similar imagery. Indeed, the same characteristics recur frequently in Faulkner's works, always more or less closely associated with his other wounded young men, like Bayard Sartoris, Horace Benbow, and Quentin Compson.

Miss Burden's house is another symbol of the synonymity of femininity and blackness: it is a "Dark House," overgrown, and apparently alive only at night, and it is a further womb image. This dual suggestion is apparent when Joe first sees the house: "The house was now dark . . . . He lay in the copse, on his belly on the dark earth. In the copse the darkness was impenetrable . . . . He could feel the neversunned earth strike, slow and receptive, against him through his clothes: groin, hip, belly, breast, forearms" (p. 215). The symbol becomes explicit when he enters the house: "he seemed to flow into the dark kitchen: a shadow returning without a sound and without locomotion to the allmother of obscurity and darkness" (p. 216). The house and the mother: those two represent a perpetual temptation for Joe, perhaps a wish to recover the paradise lost of the uterine security before the wrenching separation from the mother. That separation was in fact doubly traumatic for Joe, since his mother died in giving birth to him, and he was shortly afterwards torn from the protective love of his grandmother. He is even tempted to marry Joanna (p. 250), as he fleetingly glimpses, "instantaneous as a landscape in a lightningflash, a horizon of physical security . . . " (p. 221). He overcomes the temptation, which, if he yielded, would mean the negation of a thirty-year-long struggle to preserve his identity and his masculinity. He kills Joanna and flees from her house as he has fled from all the others where he has found a mother substitute: the orphanage, the McEacherns', the restaurant where Bobbie worked. His final refuge, the place where he chooses to die, is Hightower's house, symbolically paternal.

For Christmas, Woman is identified with blackness, in the physical and symbolic sense. Therefore she is also evil. His life has taught him that women have an affinity for evil, and inevitably cast "a faint taint of evil about the most trivial and innocent actions" (p. 157). Horace Benbow, to his horror, discovers the same trait in his daughter-in-law, and then in Temple: in despair he sees in the photograph of Little Belle "a face suddenly older in sin than he would ever be,"[6] and he vomits on his return from a visit to Temple in Memphis. This idea of women is not restricted to social outcasts. In the brilliant account of Hightower's life, as it is rumored in the town, we are told that women somehow have a sixth sense which enables them to "smell out sin" (p. 61). Mrs. Beard explains this to Byron, the innocent, whose intentions she guesses before he is aware of them himself: "'You men . . . . You can't even know your own limits for devilment. Which aint more than I can measure on a pin, at that. I reckon if it wasn't for getting some woman mixed up in it to help you, you'd ever one of you be drug hollering into heaven before you was ten years old'" (p. 396). Thus women are never innocent, for they have an instinctive feeling for evil, an affinity with the serpent, which men can only acquire after a long and gruelling initiation: Joe's story is in some sense the story of man's initiation into evil, a recurring theme in American literature. The passage from innocence to experience often leads to rebellion or despair in these characters: Joe, initially a rebel, ultimately accepts a death which is virtually a suicide, Horace Benbow is crushed and hopeless, and Quentin Compson commits suicide.

In *Light in August,* the images and symbols used to associate femininity and evil abound in great wealth—images of decay, of sewers and fearsome abysses, of thick, black, filthy water, and of death. For in Joe's eyes women are equivalent to corruption. Bobbie Allen's physical underdevelopment is linked with an inner corruption (p. 161): she has the slenderness of a child, but with huge hands and "the button eyes of a toy animal." In Joanna's case, "it was as though with the corruption which she seemed to gather from the air itself, she began to corrupt [Joe]" (p. 246). Her hair, severely tied back, makes "a knot as savage and ugly as a wart on a diseased bough" (p. 260). Most important, this old maid who has become a nymphomaniac lacks femininity. Faulkner frequently stresses her masculine attitudes and Joe himself is sufficiently astute to notice it: "She's trying to be a woman and she dont know how" (p. 227). In the end, her corruption seems masochistic: she sleeps with Joe because she believes him to be black, and in her sexual frenzy she repeats incessantly:

[*101*]

"Negro! Negro! Negro!" (p. 245), seeming to find further pleasure in her own degradation. Corruption and sterility, or at least lack of maternity, go together: the dietitian certainly does not want a child, Mrs. McEachern is childless, Bobbie is a prostitute, and Joanna at first rejects the thought of a child; when she later contemplates motherhood, probably for masochistic reasons ("A full measure. Even to a bastard negro child. I would like to see father's and Calvin's faces," p. 251), it is too late, and she mistakes her menopause for pregnancy. Doc Hines does little more than express, in a vocabulary of unprecedented violence, his grandson's own idea of women. Included with Negroes in the same hatred, women are "bitchery and abomination"; Faulkner even coins compound words compressing the two ideas into one, as in "womanfilth."

Joe's repudiation of womankind is so violent that it involves the rejection of everything associated with it. He tears from his underclothing the button sewn on by a woman, and with the cool night dew and air on his naked body he reinstates his male integrity, for coolness is, as we have seen, associated with the masculine world. His attitude toward food is also significant. Until he was caught with the toothpaste, Joe found the dietitian pleasantly suggestive, "making his mouth think of something sweet and sticky to eat" (p. 112). Afterward, food and women were linked, and he often rejects what he calls "woman's muck" (p. 225). Even when Byron offers to share his lunch with him at the mill, Joe refuses in the same contemptuous terms: "Keep your muck" (p. 31). The same association is seen in the nausea which Faulker often uses to indicate sexual revulsion. At the age of five, Joe vomits among "pinkwomansmelling" clothes, at the age of fourteen, he feels sick in the barn when he smells the Negro girl (p. 146), and when Bobbie tells him about menstruation he vomits in the woods. Altogether it seems to him that women infect everything they touch with "an odor . . . and aftertaste" of evil (p. 157). Similarly, one of Temple's friends vomits when she hears people talking of sexual intercourse, as does Horace Benbow on his return from Memphis, when he fuses Temple and Little Belle in the same fantasy of rape.[7]

At the other extreme, the masculine world is associated with cleanliness and purity, coldness and hardness. As he escapes from the warm, black moistness of female Freedman Town, Joe cannot regain self-control until he has inhaled "the cold hard air of white people" (p. 107). The white race and masculinity are classed together in their world, often characterized by the adjective "hard," which suggests that it is a world of clearly defined limits, as when Joe thinks of "the hard and ruthless justice of men" (p. 158). The word also suggests virility, for instance when Joe, horrified by the idea of menstruation, goes "among the hard trunks, . . . hardfeeling, hardsmelling" (p. 177). Finally, he surrenders himself to the "ruthless justice of men," to the hard, clean knife blade of Percy Grimm, who castrates him and thus liberates him from sexuality and women. Grimm is himself the epitome of the masculine world: deprived of the opportunity to play a part in war, that glorious man's game, he makes himself into a soldier for the preservation of order and clear-cut boundaries. To this end, he kills the Negro who has raped a white woman: "Now you'll let white women alone, even in hell" (p. 439). His reactions explain why Joe has sometimes been credited with latent homosexuality.[8] He first takes Bobbie among the phallic trees; then he becomes the lover of the masculine Joanna and struggles with her as with a man: "'My God, . . . it was like I was the woman and she was the man'" (p. 222). The night before the murder he goes to sleep in the stables, which have a reassuringly male smell: "'It's because [horses] are not women. Even a mare horse is a kind of man'" (p. 101). Joe's attitude is similar to that of Hightower, who, not understanding women, cuts himself off from them and lives with the vision of his horse-borne grandfather, a double virility symbol.

Thus, in Christmas's mind, blackness, women, and sexuality are one with evil. Even though Faulkner states that for fifteen years Joe's sexual life was conventional "as a life of healthy and normal sin usually is" (p. 246), he does not show any of it, and indeed contradicts here his earlier descriptions. During those fifteen years Joe has been seen masochistically provoking violence against himself by claiming Negro blood after sleeping with a white woman. He has even forced himself to live with a Negro woman like an ebony statue whom his whole being rejected "with physical outrage and spiritual denial" (p. 212). It seems unlikely that Joe's attitude should have been so radically different for fifteen years only to return, during his liaison with Joanna, to what it originally was with Bobbie. Either Faulkner is seeking partly to explain Joe's murder of Joanna by contrasting his relationship with her to his sexual life in the preceding fifteen years, or his account of Joe's life is meant to show him as consistently locked within a revulsion against sexuality; but then his remark on "a life of healthy and normal sin" seems somewhat out of place.

Joe's death carries a tragic significance. He seems to find the peace he has sought for thirty years only as his body grows pale with the spurting forth of "the pent black blood." For those who witness his death Joe's released blood will always evoke recaptured serenity: "It will be there, musing, quiet, steadfast, not fading and not particularly threatful, but of itself alone serene, of itself alone triumphant" (p. 440). This seems to be another image of the urn, now perfect, immutable, impervious to evil. Until this moment women were, for Joe, cracked, foul urns, and a vision of the long line of them stretching to infinity nauseated him (pp. 177-78). When he was only five, this unbearable vision was already his: he felt his nausea rising as he imagined the endless row of tubes of toothpaste he could buy with the tainted dollar offered him by the dietitian (p. 117). As the peace and whiteness of the paradise lost appear to be regained only through castration, Christmas's death may seem a horrific condemnation of sexuality. Yet, at this point, it is important to remember the ambiguity of this death.[9] It liberates Christmas from the outrage he felt when faced with life and it also in some way liberates the hidden significance of the character, making it apparent to all. His ascension raises him above himself, and while he is dead to himself, he lives on in the memory of the spectators: he becomes a myth. In his "triumph" he has regained serenity; the urn henceforth is inviolate. However, this image is not totally free of ambiguity, not only because of the unbearable and incongruous noise of the siren but also because of the cryptic glorification it implies. Such a cutting off of life in ecstasy could also manifest a horror of life and a fascination for death.

It is important to remember, however, that Joe represents only one side of the diptych. The chapters concerning him are so powerful that they tend to overshadow the importance of Lena. Yet *Light in August* begins and ends with her, and has no meaning without her. It is she who endures and prevails as the serene incarnation of eternal femininity and of the earth's fertility. On the day of Joe's death she gives birth to a child in whom he is symbolically reborn. She restores life to the sterile Burden land, as well as to Hightower, the living-dead, and to Byron, who was trying to isolate himself, working overtime at the mill to avoid the temptations of the Saturday holiday: the invincible Lena, a genuine natural force, drives the one from his impregnable ivory tower and the other from his workshop-sanctuary.

Faulkner's conception of women thus appears to be far from consistent, incorporating as it generally does the extremes of his views on the subject. The ambiguity of the characters is carried through into the themes, and much of the richness of *Light in August* is derived from the complexities and contradictions inherent in it. Woman threatens man's integrity: Joe is destroyed by Joanna, and because of his brief experience with women the convict in *The Wild Palms* returns willingly to the masculine sanctuary offered by the state prison. Yet herein lies the paradox: man can only regain his lost humanity through woman. Woman is both the destroyer and creator of life, both corrupting and redeeming.

This contradiction is, however, less serious than it seems. Lena may be supreme at the end of the novel, but she has little to do with sexuality, even while she symbolizes fertility. She is the mother, not the lover, the genetrix, not the mistress. Her relationship with Lucas Burch lasted only a very short time, and probably he was to her simply the instrument by which she could fulfill herself and obey Nature—Nature rather than her nature. It matters little whether she finds Lucas or not: when she eventually meets him, she knows that he is going to run away again. She plays with him as with a frightened animal, though without cruelty, and does nothing to hold him back. The furniture dealer understood her exactly: " 'You cant beat a woman . . . . I think she was just travelling. I dont think she had any idea of finding whoever it was she was following. I dont think she had ever aimed to, only she hadn't told him [Byron] yet' " (pp. 479-80). She will probably accept Byron in the end because without him she could not play her part in the perpetuation of fertility: *"That will be her life, her destiny. The good stock peopling in tranquil obedience to it the good earth; from these hearty loins without hurry or haste descending mother and daughter. But by Byron engendered next"* (p. 384). But as Faulkner explained at the University of Virginia, she did not really need a father for her children: "as far as she was concerned, she didn't especially need any father for [the child], any more than the women . . . on whom Jupiter begot children were anxious for a home and a father. It was enough to have had the child." [10] The queen deals with the drone as she desires: and she momentarily refuses Byron's advances.

So Lena Grove and Joanna Burden represent two

opposed concepts of womanhood, mother and mistress. In *Light in August,* Faulkner either could not or would not make a choice between them, between the glorification of Woman and the condemnation of sexuality. It seems now, in the light of this study, that the latter is possibly more important. Nurtured on the Old Testament and Christian myths, Faulkner retains the Puritan's image of Woman as the serpent and Man as the eternal Adam, striving in vain to resist the temptation of the proffered apple and to turn away from the eternal Eve. Nevertheless it is important to distinguish between two meanings of puritanism, as Faulkner does in a letter written in 1932 to Maurice E. Coindreau: "I see now that I have a quite decided strain of puritanism (in its proper sense, of course; not our American one) regarding sex. I was not aware of it."[11] In the looser sense of the word, puritanism becomes perversion, the mingled horror and fascination of the flesh as it is seen in Doc Hines, McEachern, and Joanna Burden. Christmas ultimately joins this group, but he has not always belonged to it. He sometimes does appear puritanical in the original sense of the word: that is, he is an idealist, as we shall see later on, and he has an urge toward purity which is evident in his dealings with his foster parents and in the early stages of his affair with Bobbie. Without totally misunderstanding the relationship between the author and his characters and the whole creative process, one cannot identify Faulkner with his creations and state categorically, as, for instance Maxwell Geismar has done,[12] that Woman is Evil: the role of Lena, at once structural and thematic, forbids this. Nevertheless, the great importance attached to the theme of femininity and sexuality, which exceeds that of the same theme in *The Sound and the Fury* and even in *Sanctuary* (for in contrast to these novels, here it is worked into the structure), and even more so, the amazing network of images and symbols revealing the author's mind, tend to show that Faulkner did have a puritanical sensibility in the "American" sense of the term, to use his own words.

ALIENATION AND COMPASSION

The doubt hanging over his race and his sexual revulsion are then the determining factors in Christmas's alienation. Lena, on the other hand, accepts herself as she is with no difficulty at all, and is indeed the incarnation of all that Christmas rejects. This brings us back to the fundamental opposition, evident in the structure of the novel, between the two couples, Joanna and Joe, Lena and Byron, between alienation from humanity and acceptance of it.

The alienation is, in the first place, a social one, isolation from a community: the theme of the outcast persists throughout the book. Society utterly rejects those who do not conform to its unwritten code of behavior. The community's very existence depends on its stability, for which reason it is strongly conservative, as is also seen in *Sanctuary* and *Intruder in the Dust*. Any scandal will either be smothered so that it appears not to exist, or properly punished, because while the outrage remains apparent or unchecked, it throws into doubt the community's integrity: "It was as if the very initial outrage of the murder carried in its wake and made of all subsequent actions something monstrous and paradoxical and wrong, in themselves against both reason and nature" (p. 280). The abolitionist dogmas of the Burdens menace the delicate balance of their society and so they are rejected, even destroyed if necessary. Joanna herself, devoted to the Negro cause, lives on the fringes of the community, just outside town, and the boys taunt her with the ultimate social insult: "Nigger lover." Joe's activities are known in Jefferson (he also sells moonshine whiskey) and allowed to continue until they result in open scandal. As soon as he is suspected in the murder people begin to talk freely, and the news that he has black blood unifies local opinion. They have nothing against him personally, but he must be expunged from the community according to their rites, and he must accept the punishment too. Animosity toward him is only bred when he defies their code at Mottstown: "He never acted like either a nigger or a white man. That was it. That was what made the folks so mad. . . . It was like he never knew he was a murderer, let alone a nigger too" (p. 331).

The Hightower affair throws even more light on the attitude of the community. The ladies of the parish performed their social duty, and were attentive to the minister as long as his wife conformed to their code and maintained at least the appearance of respectability. When she went back to Memphis and stopped going to church, the ladies ignored her, and tried to forget her existence, which was in itself a defiance and an outrage to them. When the scandal finally broke out, the people in Jefferson used every means at their disposal, including violence, to expel Hightower. In the end, when they had done all that was expected of them in this closed society (p. 66), and Hightower still remained, they ignored him as a unit of society and, paradoxically, felt at liberty to offer charity to this pariah now living outside their order.

Conversely, the community accepts Lena, who, in spite of her pregnancy, does not challenge the social order, or do anything other than what is expected of her. Lena settles easily in Jefferson, where everyone helps her at one time or another: Mrs. Armstid, Mrs. Beard, the doctor, Hightower himself, the sheriff, the furniture dealer, and, of course, Byron, her knight errant. Mrs. Beard tells Byron the general feeling: "Ain't you and that preacher and ever other man that knows about her already done everything for her that she could think to want?" (p. 397).

Social pressure is not the only cause of an individual's alienation, nor is it the most important. Such pressure is usually applied from the outside, by a community which remains anonymous. In *Light in August*, we see above all isolated people, condemned to solitude by society perhaps, but primarily because they have rejected the humanity within themselves as well as around them. They have done so because of their past, or because of their lack of past, which comes to the same thing. Hightower is haunted by the feeling that he was dead before ever he was born, for he died, so he thinks, when his grandfather was killed on his return from a cavalry charge through Jefferson. As a result, he attempts to recover this former life by re-creating it in a sanctuary of dreams, from which he excludes all living things, thus causing the death of his wife. He is a hostage of the dead, as only Byron understands: " 'it's the dead folks that do him the damage. It's the dead ones that lay quiet in one place and dont try to hold him, that he cant escape from' " (p. 69). Joanna Burden, too, is the prisoner of a grandfather and a half-brother killed during the Reconstruction. Ever since her father took her to see their graves and delivered her a terrifying sermon on the reciprocal curse between the black and white races, she has been bound to this past, which has become a personal nightmare, preventing her from ever attaining a living relationship with the present. She denies her femininity and becomes masculine: her final attempt to be a woman fails because she uses Joe as an instrument without recognizing him as a human being in his own right. Even Percy Grimm is obsessed by a past which he was born too late to experience. He counteracts this disappointment by building himself a dreamworld of nationalism and racism, where human beings have no place beyond their usefulness as pawns on a board.

Joe struggles with the enigma of his birth. He does not know who he is: he is nobody's son, therefore he is nobody. He has no name of his own; he is a shadow, a ghost among shadows. His torment lies in the uncertainty which he knows he can never resolve, as a Negro at the orphanage tells him brutally: " 'You are worse than that [a nigger]. You dont know what you are. And more than that, you wont never know. You'll live and you'll die and you wont never know,'" (p. 363). Whether he has black blood or not does not affect the issue: his is a psychological and social problem, not a biological one. Joe Christmas is a man in search of his identity, and his search is doomed to failure. He was born into a violent world, and subsequently deprived of all tenderness. All his life he has been manipulated, first by the dietitian, and later by Brown, both of whom had to extricate themselves from dangerous situations. Joanna used him to satisfy her sexual cravings, and then to appease her conscience. Hines and McEachern both used him as an object for the divine wrath of which each felt himself to be the chosen agent. So the only weapons Joe knows are defiance and violence, and he uses them to assert himself. Over and over again, he rejects, rebels, strikes, kills. The twenty-four hours before the crime, in chapter 5, are the final culminating repetition of all his former repudiations. And he kills Joanna when she tries to impose upon him an identity which would for him represent a limitation, even a negation, of his whole life, for he would be definitively accepted as a Negro. The final provocation is her threatening him with a pistol, dating, symbolically enough, from the Civil War. His violence is even a provocation in itself, as if he hoped that the blows received would define him. Eventually he chooses the only certainty, his own destruction, perhaps thinking that death will give him an identity and a place among humanity: his is one of the henceforth peaceful faces in Hightower's vision.

That Joe is a rebel is ultimately due to the fact that he is a disappointed idealist. He finds it unbearable that division, limitation, imperfection, and impurity should exist in man, and that the flesh should subjugate man to the rhythms of Nature. He seeks an impossible perfection, as is shown by the idyllic quality of his love for, ironically, a prostitute. His violence is his reaction against human limitations, his revolt a refusal to accept the human condition and the bitter fruit of knowledge. Indeed, his alienation springs in part from the fact that each new experience leads him further from self-knowledge and self-acceptance instead of nearer to them, divides the elements of his character instead of harmonizing them, so much so that during his affair with Joanna he is really a white by day, and a Negro by night. His uniform of black trousers and white shirt is a perfect image of the dichotomy in his personality. This then is Christmas's tragedy: it is not that he is always fatally driven to refuse and reject, but rather that he has been so formed, and deformed, by his experiences that violence and defiance are his only means of self-assertion. His fidelity to himself and to his dignity as a man are ironically the causes of his isolation. Thus he resists the various attempts made on him by women because they involve limitation and threaten his integrity; similarly, he refuses to identify himself with either race, although he does so, temporarily at least, as though in spite of himself.[13]

So *Light in August* is not a novel in the school of Naturalism, where hereditary and environmental factors exclusively mold the characters. Hightower cuts himself off from humanity by choice, as Byron reminds him. Christmas believes himself free when he has resisted the temptation to marry Joanna: " 'No. If give in now, I will deny all the thirty years that I have lived to make me what I chose to be' " (pp. 250–51). Every choice poses for him a dilemma, accepting and renouncing his idea of integrity, or refusing and being ever more divided within himself and alienated from humanity: the choices are there for all that. So Joe paradoxically manages to retain a narrow area of freedom within the imprisoning circle: "he believed with calm paradox that he was the volitionless servant of the fatality in which he believed that he did not believe" (p. 264). That he should use this freedom to try to overcome the difficulties besetting him and to affirm his dignity (as neither Popeye nor the contemptible Brown, the parody of a "disciple," do) gives him his grandeur in Faulkner's eyes. That is how the author preserves his, and our, admiration for an otherwise totally unsympathetic character: "He knew that he would never know what he was, and his only salvation in order to live with himself was to repudiate mankind, to live outside the human race . . . that to me is the most tragic condition that an individual can have."[14]

All the alienated beings are alone. The theme of the solitary individual cut off from common values and common humanity recurs persistently in modern literature. It is usually set in big cities, as in Dreiser's works, where the loneliness and isolation of man in modern urban society is a major concern. By pursuing this theme against a poor and simple small-town background, where the word "community" still means something, Faulkner intensifies the hopelessness of man's situation and the tragedy of his solitude. In *Light in August,* the generally anonymous community is the background against which the essentially solitary people stand out: Byron at the beginning, Hightower, and Doc Hines; even the young Percy Grimm has nobody to whom he can talk freely (p. 426); and the solitude of Joe and Joanna is unchanged when they become lovers, for they rarely talk to each other and remain total strangers.

The theme of noncommunication, the real leitmotiv of *As I Lay Dying,* appears now and then in *Light in August.* The characters neither hear nor understand each other. Words, which should be the means of communication, are meaningless, "just a shape to fill a lack," as Addie Bundren thinks. They are invented by those who refuse life, and for whom they replace experience.[15] Joanna's greed for words is significant: she is really in love with love (or with the word-symbol abstractions) rather than with a unique and irreplaceable human individual, upon whom she can only impose an identity which suits her own needs (pp. 244, 262). Words are screens which hide and replace reality, as Hightower thinks, paraphrasing Hamlet: "'But there are more things in heaven and earth too than truth. . . . More things indeed,' thinking how ingenuity was apparently given man in order that he may supply himself in crises with shapes and sounds with which to guard himself from truth" (p. 453). Byron does not truly return to life when he falls in love with Lena, who is then only the *object* of his passion: his resurrection, so to speak, only occurs when he hears the cry of her child and realizes that Lucas Burch and Lena are people of flesh and blood, and not just names, abstractions, and thus, too, that Lena is no longer a virgin: *"It was like me, and her, and all the other folks that I had to get mixed up in it, were just a lot of words that never even stood for anything, were not even us, while all the time what was us was going on and going on without even missing the lack of words"* (p. 380).

While Christmas represents alienation, violence, and sterility, Lena is a fulfilled being, accepting Nature and fertility. Perfectly at ease wherever she goes, finding everyone "right kind," she has an instinctive sense of solidarity—often recognizing it shrewdly in others. There is no sign in her of the mutilation or perversion of nature: unlike other characters, her face never hardens into a mask of pain or rage. She propagates herself instead of destroying herself. She has no need to search for an identity: elemental, in complete harmony with the earth, she is Nature itself. She is neither obsessed with nor corrupted by evil: rather she represents the purity and innocence of prelapsarian man. She is thus a measure of the alienation of others, occupying a strategic position in the structure of the novel. Faulkner's frequent expressions of his admiration for Lena[16] have their source in his view of her as the incarnation of those truths of the heart he mentioned in his Stockholm address, "the old verities and truths of the heart, the old universal truths lacking which any story is ephemeral and doomed— love and honor and pity and pride and compassion and sacrifice."[17] Lena may not be totally unambiguous, and her qualities may sometimes seem purely instinctive, but she nevertheless possesses them, be it only negatively.

The qualities which give man his grandeur, which enable him to endure and to prevail are then those of the heart, not of the mind, as Hightower discovers at the conclusion of his passion. He has repudiated his heart to live entirely in a mentally created world which no one else may enter. He has therefore repudiated the whole of humanity, so that he is as guilty as Ethan Brand in Hawthorne's tale. All his life, he has shielded himself from human suffering in his church as well as in his home and immunized himself against compassion as though against a disease. He has never felt anything but contempt for this ridiculous animal, man: as he sees the Hineses through his window they remind him of bears, and, as he thinks, chuckling to himself, Byron lacks only a handkerchief on his head and a pair of earrings (p. 348). A few days earlier he had had a Swiftian vision of Byron, "moving with that precarious and meretricious cleverness of animals balanced on their hinder legs; that cleverness of which the man animal is so fatuously proud and which constantly betrays him by means of natural laws like gravity and ice, . . . and the very refuse of his own eating left upon floor or pavement" (p. 70). The horse (inseparable from the image of his grandfather, who is also his god) then seemed to him superior to Man. Such scorn and hatred inevitably remind one of Gulliver in the land of the Houyhnhnms.

Turning his back on suffering humanity, Hightower sought refuge in the Church. He thought that it would be an ideal retreat, where, far from men, he would be able to construct a perfect existence for himself: "it seemed to him that he could see his future, his life, intact and on all sides complete and inviolable, like a classic and serene vase" (p. 453). Would not such an image appear to suggest the appreciation of an aesthete, antithetical in itself to the religious vocation? So Hightower became one of those professionals of the Church "who have removed the bells from its steeples" and who have used it as "a rampart . . . against truth and against that peace in which to sin and be forgiven which is the life of man" (p. 461). This oft-quoted phrase is perhaps one of the most important in the whole novel. The crux of the scandal is there: that the Church is no longer a rampart for the protection of the afflicted, but instead constitutes a barrier *against* them. *Light in August* appears as a terrible denunciation of a religion which preaches the opposite of truth and the forgiveness of sins; of a Church which has become the negation of its own raison d'être. The implacable music of the organ which Hightower hears through his window is the image of such a religion, "pleading, asking, for not love, not life, forbidding it to others, demanding in sonorous tones death as though death were the boon" (p. 347). In fact, religion as it is seen in *Light in August* becomes an incitement to kill: it is completely orientated towards death. For McEachern and Doc Hines forgiveness is just as obscene as sin, and the death of the sinner is the only way to eradicate the sin. Miss Burden is apparently prepared to kill Joe, the instrument of her sin, and then to kill herself. And before Hightower eventually opens his heart to compassion and the love of his neighbor, he has caused his wife's death in the name of a religion which allowed him to merge in scandalous confusion the images of Christ, dying on the cross, full of forgiveness, and of his own grandfather, killed after a destructive raid in Jefferson as he pillaged a hen house (p. 462).

If one looks only at the important characters in the present of the novel, one is forced to conclude that those four are the only ones to show any real religious convictions. It is safe to assume that Byron is an orthodox Christian, "a kind of Protestant Everyman," [18] but the only certainty in relation to him, the only proof that he holds any such convictions, is that he travels thirty miles on his mule every Saturday evening to lead the choir in a country church. However, it must be added that, as a good Protestant, he should regard idleness as the root of all evil: and every Saturday afternoon he works, alone, to avoid temptation. Also, it is impossible to forget that he felt pity for Christmas's grandparents, and that he tried to save Joe from the vengeful ire of the public by asking Hightower to establish an alibi for him. [19] As for Joe, he has repudiated everything related to religion; the fanaticism of McEachern and of Miss Burden horrifies him. And it is surely significant that Lena, the only character in the book truly in harmony with Nature and the rest of humanity, should also be the most completely nonreligious of all. Her serenity is not the result of faith. In *Light in August,* therefore, one sees mostly examples of perverted religion; that is, religion which practices, and even preaches, exactly the opposite of what it should represent.

Terrible as this is, such a condemnation is not, as we know, the last word of the novel. Hightower confesses his guilt, and his last thought, as the wheel of his vision turns on and away, recognizes the sufferings of humanity (p. 466). Compassion, or love (the two are often synonymous for Faulkner), is the one quality of the heart which encompasses all the others—the only one which can redeem and save man. That is one of Faulkner's main themes, and a great many of his major works show the disastrous consequences of a lack of love: all that remains of the Compson dynasty is an emasculated idiot and his ridiculed brother who is a prey to impotent fury, because there has been no love in the family; and we see the fall of the house of Sutpen because Thomas Sutpen's "innocence" is nothing but the result of disproportionate pride overruling the heart, and a complete inability to understand the reasons of the heart.

Yet the thread of irony running through *Light in August*

throws doubt on the real significance of the novel. In the end, only Lena and Byron continue their journey and show the victory of life and love, in the same way as Dilsey and Cash Bundren. Yet, like Cash, Lena and Byron are comic figures. Byron, " 'the kind of fellow you wouldn't see the first glance if he was alone by himself in the bottom of a empty concrete swimming pool' " (p. 469), is very puppetlike at the end; and Lena, bovine as ever, leaves Jefferson as though nothing of any import had ever occurred, and watches the telegraph poles going past "like it was a circus parade" (p. 480). It is ironic that the characters possessed of admirable qualities should leave a comic impression, just as it is ironic that Hightower, ugly, shapeless, repulsive, and inspiring the same aversion as he had felt, should represent universal compassion. Similarly, it is incongruous that fanatics like Doc Hines, McEachern, and Percy Grimm should succeed, infallibly guided, in their pursuit, and that Hightower, the man of God, should be unable to save the profane and sacrilegious Joe, who himself becomes the involuntary agent of Hightower's probable salvation. And although Joe's revolt is hardly promethean, and leads only to sterility and death, Faulkner undoubtedly admires the intransigence of the man, his refusal to compromise, which gives him a dignity never achieved by Brown, his ironic double; in addition, the chapters concerning him are so important and powerful that he dominates all the other characters.

It seems that in *Light in August* Faulkner neither wished, nor was able, to reconcile the evil, violence, and suffering he saw on earth with the love he pleaded for. Neither does he reconcile his tragic vision of the human condition with his desire to believe in a future for man. The tensions remain, and it is not until the advent of the admirable character Nancy Mannigoe, in *Requiem for a Nun,* that the redeeming value of suffering is unequivocally asserted.

6

Stylistic Approaches

FAULKNER PROBABLY HAD LITTLE MORE CONFIDENCE than his contemporaries in a language made up of words deprived of meaning ("words are no good; . . . words dont ever fit even what they are trying to say at," thinks Addie Bundren),[1] which rarely help communication and often prevent it altogether. However, he did try to make this inadequate tool work for him by evoking in the reader's mind images and emotions which would correspond as nearly as possible to his own mental vision: "One of the great ironies in Faulkner is the creation of experiential truth . . . out of words which are in themselves held to be insufficient to convey or embody truth."[2] Though little significant criticism has yet been written on this aspect of Faulkner's art, the critics are generally agreed in attributing to him two sorts of style. One is sober and accurate, describing with rare felicity light and sounds, outlines and movements, remarkably vivid sensory impressions. The other is rich, expansive, sonorous, imaginative, and interpretative, exploring all the possibilities of language, setting aside rules and conventions, spanned and harmonized by immense movements of prose—to talk of sentences would be out of place—of which the most remarkable and consistent example is *Absalom, Absalom!* This rhetoric is the most controversial aspect of Faulkner's art. Even though *Light in August* and

Absalom, Absalom! are not written in the same style, that of the former has a power and a beauty which, however, far exceed the descriptive style.

The style of *Light in August* is indeed difficult to define. By comparison it is easier to analyze Faulkner's rhetoric, which, in its occasionally unbearable excess, reveals its methods. In *Light in August* the rhetoric never really intrudes except perhaps briefly in the reflections on Joanna's death (p. 273). Likewise, grammatical gymnastics are rare (in the sentence "It was the woman who . . .," p. 157, the relative pronoun is not followed by a verb), as are those long parentheses which suspend the sentence so that the reader may simultaneously perceive everything the author wishes him to absorb. Polysyllabic latinate words, which, at their best, are rich in connotations both precise and abstract, and which give a unique sonority and rhythm to parts of "The Bear" and *Absalom, Absalom!,* are sparingly used, and the same is true of rare or precious words like "banshee," "Juggernaut," "suttee," and such adjectives as "promptive," "abnegant," "maculate," "punctuate."

Before defining and illustrating the actual qualities of Faulkner's style in this novel, we must first say how conscious and conscientious a craftsman he is. The useful romantic image of a Faulkner driven by his demons and writing in a trance (or indeed in a haze of bourbon) hardly corresponds to the truth. As Faulkner himself has explained in the autobiographical passage of 1933 quoted in the first chapter of this study, *Light in August,* no more than any of the other novels after *The Sound and the Fury,* was not written with the urgency which characterized the 1929 masterpiece. Even though, as we have shown, the author felt some indecision in planning the architecture of the novel, he nevertheless insists in this text on the *deliberation* with which he wrote it, and on the overawareness, due to his thorough knowledge of his trade, which prevented him from being carried away by inspiration. Anyone who has studied Faulkner's manuscripts and typescripts is necessarily made aware of the meticulous care which he gave to the details of composition and writing.

The manuscript of *Light in August* has already been discussed in chapter 1. It is remarkable that apart from the pasted-up passages, particularly numerous in the first half, this manuscript has very few corrections. The writing, in the passages between these collages, is so hurried that often the ends of words are missing and the text is occasionally illegible. Such haste could lead one to suppose that the author was in fact copying from a previous script, correcting it as he went along: that would explain why there are so few visible alterations, not counting the paste-ups. On the other hand, a great many minor changes, mostly stylistic, were made when the novel was being typed out, although there are no visible signs of them. Short insertions, revised or new sentences, and indeed a few long passages seem to have emerged ready-made from the author's mind to take their place in the final text. Often, it is only through a comparison of the two texts that one may appreciate his sure sense of rhythm and sound (in several places, words or groups of words which are repeated were so arranged only during the typing of the text), and the precision with which the vocabulary is gradually adjusted to correspond with the author's concept. The slightest details, of spelling, punctuation, quotation marks, even of spacing, command his meticulous attention.

There is one document which forcefully shows these qualities in Faulkner: the galley proofs of the novel, now in the possession of the Humanities Research Center of the University of Texas at Austin. The copy editor at Smith and Haas several times took it upon himself to suggest "improvements." Faulkner's comments, haughty or annoyed, sometimes furious, are those of a writer admirably sure of himself and confidently refusing to change any part of a text whose every detail he had already carefully pondered. (He would only agree to alter obvious errors.) For instance, the astonishing opening paragraph of chapter 6 seemed rather unorthodox to the copy editor, who wrote in the margin: "construction?"—to which Faulkner replied: "O.K. damn it" (galley 33). On reading this phrase: "He saw now that the cabin sat some two feet above the earth" (p. 437), the editor feared there was some mistake and suggested "set, instead of sat"—which drew the following from Faulkner: "I dont think that 'set' is a very good verb. Thanks, though" (galley 128). Some grammar "mistakes" in the furniture dealer's account were apparently unacceptable: "Then he came back, with enough wood to barbecue a steer, and she began to tell him and he went to the truck and taken out that suitcase and opened it and taken out a blanket" (p. 473). The editor proposed changing "taken," which is perfectly normal in this character's speech, to "took" in each case, at which Faulkner became angry: "No, damn it!!! O.K. as set" (galley 138). Likewise, Calvin Burden's vocabulary in this threat to his son surprised the copy editor: "'I'll learn you to hate two things, . . . or I'll frail the tar out of you'" (p. 229). But Faulkner refused to change "frail" to "flail," an alteration which would have diluted the verbal vigor and dimmed the color of his character: "O.K. as set and written. Jesus Christ" (galley 67). Finally, as a last example of the care he took to preserve the full flavor of dialects in the spoken word, there is this thought of Byron: "'I be dog if it dont look like a man that has done as much lying lately as I have . . .'" (p. 374), which the copy editor questioned tentatively: "Expression O.K.?"—at which Faulkner's annoyance erupted: "O.K. Why in hell not?" (galley 129). These few examples, selected from among many others, conclusively show that the author of *Light in August* was a writer perfectly sure of his methods and master of his language.

PRECISION

The first remarkable qualities of the style in *Light in August* are its precision and sobriety—especially remarkable if the novel is compared with the later ones. For the most part Faulkner uses relatively short sentences which are easy to understand and which concentrate on reporting accurately the movements, words, and thoughts of the characters. Such precise descriptive methods give an impression of objectivity, sometimes reminiscent of Hemingway's style, where the author effaces himself so that the reader feels as though he has apprehended *immediately* the objects or actions described or reported. This effect is seen, for instance, in the description of Lena awaiting Armstid's wagon, then climbing into it and sitting by his side, of the brusque Mrs. Armstid in her kitchen and bedroom, of Byron at work, of Christmas methodically striking Brown, and of his every deed and gesture during the twenty-four hours before the murder. The description of Joe at dawn on the Friday when he decides to give himself up is a particularly good example of this minute precision:

> It is just dawn, daylight. He rises and descends to the spring and takes from his pocket the razor, the brush, the soap. But it is still too dim to see his face clearly in the water, so he sits beside the spring and waits until he can see better. Then he lathers his face with the hard, cold water, patiently. His hand trembles, despite the urgency he feels a lassitude so that he must drive himself. The razor is dull; he tries to whet it upon the side of one brogan, but the leather is ironhard and wet with dew. He shaves, after a fashion. His hand trembles; it is not a very good job, and he cuts himself three or four times, stanching the blood with the cold water until it stops. He puts the shaving tools away and begins to walk. [pp. 317-18]

The quality of the style here lies in the fact that the exact verb is the energy or the muscle of each sentence. Adjectives and adverbs are few, and apart from the adjective "hard," used twice, and which at this place in the novel is charged with suggestions of Joe's aversion to femininity insofar as it denies his masculinity, and the repetition of the phrase "his hand trembles," the passage is entirely objective, apparently a camera view of the character. Yet the minute precision does not mean that the reader has a detached view: on the contrary, this graphic prose, which does not seek to involve the reader with violent images or powerful rhythms, forces him instead to participate directly in the actions by an almost physical contact. Karl Zink has remarked on this: "This prose too has its own compulsive immediacy. . . . It becomes almost a literal transcript of action alone and . . . compels empathy, a kind of motor mimicry."[3]

The spoken word in *Light in August* is a further illustration of the precision of Faulkner's style. Whether in dialogue or in the narrators' accounts, each character has a voice which, in some cases, is easily distinguishable since it renders the personal inflections and rhythms, the idiosyncrasies of vocabulary, the regional colloquialisms, and the common errors of speech suggesting a certain social class. Hines, for instance, is unbelievable; it is unthinkable that he should preach in Negro churches the supremacy of the white race. Yet as soon as one hears his demented speech he becomes credible. His unique vocabulary, crystallizing his biblico-sexual obsessions, has already been mentioned. And Faulkner admirably succeeds in containing the violence and the colloquialisms within biblical cadences:

> he saw that young doctor coming in lechery and fornication stop and stoop down and raise the Lord's abomination and tote it into the house. And old Doc Hines he followed and he seen and heard. He watched them young sluts that was desecrating the Lord's sacred anniversary with eggnog and whiskey in the Madam's absence, open the blanket. And it was her, the Jezebel of the doctor, that was the Lord's instrument, that said, 'We'll name him Christmas' . . . . [p. 363]

The long sonorous latinisms, charged with religious connotations, reinforce the regularity of the binary and sometimes ternary rhythm of the phrases: "lechery . . . fornication," "stop . . . stoop," "raise . . . tote," "fornication . . . abomination," "followed . . . seen . . . heard," "desecrating . . . sacred," "eggnog . . . whiskey." This richly rhythmic language with the severe authority of the Bible and a long tradition of threatening sermons in the background never loses its colloquial flavor ("tote," "Doc Hines he followed," "he seen," "them young sluts that was desecrating"). Lena too is recognizable by her local dialect (double negatives, wrong verb forms), by her country style, which still retains archaic forms ("unbeknownst," "a-going," "a-walking"), and by expressions and pronunciations peculiar to the South ("right kind," "right far," "a fur piece," "I et polite"). Even the furniture dealer has the rich imaginative speech of the countryman, which leads him to describe Byron as "the kind of fellow you wouldn't see the first glance if he was alone by himself in the bottom of a empty concrete swimming pool," and Lena's baby as "a critter not yearling size" (p. 469).

There is no really striking difference between the spoken and the narrative language in *Light in August*. As already seen, it is largely a difference of intensity rather than of quality, and the characteristics of the style outlined here are found in the dialogue as well as in the narrative of the omniscient author. Moreover, Faulkner often integrates the dialogue and the descriptions so that they form an inseparable whole: a fair number of corrections from the manuscript to the typescript work toward this end, as the author changed some descriptive sentences to spoken ones, blurring the distinctions between his own comments and those of his characters, as can be seen in a comparison of the original and final texts of the first description of Christmas. Here is the manuscript: "He looked like a tramp. Not a professional hobo in the professional rags, but like a man down on his luck and not intending to stay down on it for long and not particularly caring how he rose above it." In the published book, the first part of this description, considerably extended and made more suggestive of the character's spiritual rootlessness, is still ascribed to the omniscient author, while the second half becomes actual speech:

> "As if," as the men said later, "he was just down on his luck for a time, and that he didn't intend to stay down on it and didn't give a damn much how he rose up." [p. 27]

Such unobstrusive inclusion of spoken language makes the description more vivid and the gradual revelation of the character more natural, as the reader's knowledge of Christmas parallels that of his fellow workers; thus the reader is not left with a merely personal, possibly unwarranted, impression of the character, as it is shared by witnesses whose unmistakably living speech retrospectively gives a ring of truth to the whole paragraph. In a similar way, when typing the novel, Faulkner changed some narrative sentences into his characters' own thoughts. For instance, the first of Lena's reflections in italics on page 6 read in the manuscript: "Then it would be as though she were riding for a half mile . . ."; and Christmas's thoughts on pages 98 and 99: "*I have been in bed now since ten o'clock . . .*," and "*Perhaps that is where outrage lies . . .*," were likewise in the third person. A comparison of the manuscript and the published book reveals that in the final text Faulkner often achieved a closer integration of the third-person narration with spoken language or unspoken thoughts, thus making his narrative more dramatic and his characters more vividly perceived and better endowed with an inner, brooding sort of life.

INTENSITY

The language of *Light in August* has an intensity deriving from what we may call at once accretion and compression.

Even more than James Fenimore Cooper, Faulkner would have earned Mark Twain's censure, particularly because of his almost inordinate use of adjectives. Yet he succeeds in accumulating them to such a degree that they carry the whole emotional weight of a given passage. Lena is summed up, morally as well as physically, in only five adjectives: "swollen, slow, deliberate, unhurried and tireless" (p. 7). In the manuscript the first was "pregnant"; the alteration replaces the abstract term by a word which is not only more graphic but which also adds alliteration and assonance. On his arrival at Mrs. Beard's, Byron's voice is described by three adjectives with Latin roots, which, by the repetition of the same consonants, suggest the character's feverish insistence. In each case, the stress falls on the first or central syllable, and the final syllables, heavy and muffled, somehow evoke the impotence Byron felt in face of the situation: "recapitulant, urgent, importunate" (p. 78). McEachern, too, is contained in the adjectival accretion qualifying him as he takes home the child he has just adopted: "The man was bundled too against the cold, squat, big, shapeless, somehow rocklike, indomitable, not so much ungentle as ruthless" (p. 135). The respective attitudes of Joanna and Joe are concentrated in a few well-chosen adjectives, in the description of their confrontation during the third phase of their relationship: "Their faces were not a foot apart: the one cold, dead white, fanatical, mad; the other parchmentcolored, the lip lifted into the shape of a soundless and rigid snarl" (p. 262). Finally, Hightower's house is described in the following series of adjectives: "the house unpainted, small, obscure, poorly lighted, mansmelling, manstale" (p. 44). When this is compared with the manuscript version ("the small, poorly lighted, manstale house were the ex-minister lives with what the town calls his disgrace") it is obvious that Faulkner has moved the adjectives to the end of the sentence to lay greater stress upon them, and that two of the added adjectives ("obscure" and "mansmelling"), far from being synonymous with the others, add shades of meaning, and enlarge the vision by evoking Hightower himself and his whole existence as well as his house.

Faulkner is not satisfied with the accretion of adjectives alone (in fact, the technique is used with restraint here compared to later works): he also tries to exploit the adjectives themselves to their full potential, in particular widening their range of application by making them sylleptic—in a loose way. For instance, in describing Lena's journey, he uses such expressions as "anonymous and deliberate wagons," "steady and unflagging hypnosis" (p. 5), or "the red and unhurried miles" (p. 25): "anonymous" refers rather to the drivers than to the wagons, and "deliberate" to Lena herself; "steady and unflagging" actually describes the mules' pace, "red" the road surface rather than an abstract distance, and "unhurried" the movement of the wagons. The first example quoted, "anonymous and deliberate wagons," differs from the manuscript, which reads: "anonymous and slow." The alteration clearly illustrates Faulkner's concern to give his adjectives the greatest possible extension. (The word "deliberate" thus appears once more in this first chapter, in which it always characterizes the attitude of the young woman.) Again, as she sits on the steps of the Varner store, Lena remembers her breakfast, "the decorous morsel of strange bread" (p. 23): "decorous" in fact describes Lena's manners not the morsel, and "strange," the Armstid family. The word "morsel" itself adds to the impression of strangeness and gives the remembered scene an added dimension of eternity, removing it from its specific, rather mundane, context, and making it into an experience no longer unique. In the same way, "deliberate" describes McEachern's whole attitude rather than the strap or the noise of the blows he deals: "the strap . . . rose and fell, deliberate, numbered, with deliberate, flat reports" (p. 150); "dying," "spent," and "satiate" evoke the lassitude of lovers whose passion has waned: "they would be stranded as behind a dying mistral, upon a spent and satiate beach" (p. 248); and "hurried" refers to the women themselves, not their clothes: "in bright and sometimes hurried garments" (p. 273). Sometimes, too, the process is reversed, and the meaning of the adjective slides, not from subject to object as in most of the examples just quoted, but from object to subject: *"the ladies constant and a little sibilant with fans"* (p. 346). This stylistic mannerism has many effects. Disregarding the rules of grammar, the adjective hangs suspended between subject and object, referring to either or both, thus preventing analytical developments. This use of ellipsis is one way of compressing and intensifying language. In addition, it forces the reader to look at people and objects in a new light, breaking through the traditional perceptions and language forms. This is turn contributes to the immediacy of the style (as in "the slow buttocks of mules," p. 192). In the end, adjectives so used become sufficient in themselves to evoke the character or the emotion they originally qualified.

The effort toward the compression of language in *Light in August* is again apparent in the invention of a great number of compound words. The compound nouns are most frequently connected with Christmas, Doc Hines, and Hightower, almost shaping into language their obsessions and their rigid conception of a world where male and female are in a constant struggle for mastery. The most remarkable of these words do in fact begin with "man" and even more often with "woman": "maneyes," "manodor," "manshape," "manvoice," "womenvoices," "womangarments," "womanfilth," "womansinning," "womanevil," "womanshenegro," and so on. The compound adjectives, elliptical and vividly suggestive, are even more numerous than the nouns. They either concentrate an obsession into a single word that makes it felt at once, physically, as in "fecundmellow," "pinkfoamed," "pinkwomansmelling," "hardsmelling," "deathcolored," or they stand for an entire description, as in the case of "bugswirled," "heelgnawed," "stumppocked," "hookwormridden," "pinewiney," "August-tremulous," "patinasmooth," "cinderstrewnpacked," "thwart-facecurled." Their power of suggestion is often increased by the combination of precise concrete terms with abstract ones, giving them a timeless significance, beyond that of the particular context in which they appear, as in "diamond-surfaced respectability," "creakwheeled and limpeared avatars," "softungirdled presence," "shadowbrooded," "branchshadowed quiet," "stillwinged and tremulous suspension."

Faulkner also makes frequent use of oxymorons, which, by juxtaposing contradictory terms, give a strange impression of a reality that remains forever in a state of suspension while at the same time striking the reader's imagination by its contradictory aspects, making him share and feel rather than judge and understand. One typically Faulknerian example of this technique is "slow and terrific"; others in this novel include: "the wagon crawls terrifically," "terrific . . . idleness," "motionless wheels rising," "fumbling and interminable haste," "fields and woods . . . at once static and fluid," "[Hightower's] face is at once gaunt and flabby," or "[Joe's] feet seemed to stray . . . at deliberate random." As in the case of the frequent negative forms previously mentioned, the oxymorons prevent the substitution of language and logic for experience and emotion, as Walter J. Slatoff explains: "so long as our reactions are in a suspension rather than in crystallized form, they remain feelings and experiences rather than rational or verbal constructions."[4]

The density of the style is further enhanced by an economy of punctuation. Faulkner often accretes his adjectives without separating them by commas: "The hot still pinewiney silence of the August afternoon" (p. 5; the adjectives are still separated in the manuscript), "the lightless hot wet primogenitive Female" (p. 107), "a big long garbled cold echoing building of dark red brick . . . , set in a grassless cinderstrewnpacked compound . . ." (p. 111). The whole paragraph of which this is part is a remarkable demonstration of the effects Faulkner can achieve through the absence of punctuation. These desolate, sinister images of the orphanage, the prison in which love-starved children are caged, are not quite assimilated separately although read in succession. Together they combine to produce a uniquely intense emotion so much more violent than would be the sum of the minor emotions aroused by each individual image. Thus, these unpunctuated image series are a more sophisticated development of the compound word—for which Faulkner never uses hyphens in this novel. To join all these words together into one would only result in confusion, but by dispensing with all superfluous punctuation Faulkner makes clear his intention.

RHYTHM

Rhythm also contributes to the power of the prose in *Light in August*. The pulsations throbbing through the sentences and rhythmically extending from one to another virtually destroy the sentence as a unit of prose, even though the general impression of the novel remains one of measured syntax. Indeed, the author never entangles the reader in inordinately long periods, which dull his faculties of analysis and abstraction, drugging him into a state of receptivity so that he may respond *immediately* to rhythm and to the suggestive power of images. Nevertheless, a similar effect is more subtly and effectively achieved here by the rhythmic undulations which overflow and drown the formal sentence. This observation is substantiated if one listens to Faulkner reading aloud (there are some recordings), in prolonged, monotonous rhythms which more often than not do not correspond to the syntactical divisions. In this novel the rhythm is largely dictated by the repetitions of words (which often do not yet occur to such an extent in the manuscript stage of the text), by the interplay of sonorities, and by the studied alternation of strong and weak beats.

The first illustrative passage is interesting because it appears on the surface to be completely straightforward, with nothing outstanding in its vocabulary: its suggestive power is solely derived from the rhythm. It recounts the life of the workers in the planing mill and their attitudes on Monday morning after the weekend break:

> Some of the other workers were family men and some were bachelors and they were of different ages and they led a catholic variety of lives, yet on Monday morning they all came to work with a kind of gravity, almost decorum. Some of them were young, and they drank and gambled on Saturday night, and even went to Memphis now and then. Yet on Monday morning they came quietly and soberly to work, in clean overalls and clean shirts, waiting quietly until the whistle blew and then going quietly to work, as though there were still something of Sabbath in the overlingering air which established a tenet that, no matter what a man had done with his Sabbath, to come quiet and clean to work on Monday morning was no more than seemly and right to do. [pp. 36-37]

The first sentence (one has to use the term for reference purposes) begins with four statements, in pairs ("some . . . were . . . and some were," "and they were . . . and they led"), and each pair has seven strong beats alternating fairly regularly with weak beats. Then the rhythm changes as a new idea is introduced, still in the same sentence: "yet on Monday morning they all came to work," and this idea is taken up again two sentences later in almost the same form. The sentence terminates with two complementary words, "gravity" and "decorum," both of Latin root, both with an unstressed ending, matching the subdued attitude of the workers, and their wish to pass unnoticed. The next sentence echoes the beginning of the first ("some of them") in three propositions which expand progressively from three to five strong beats. The beginning of the third sentence takes up the second part of the first and, in an almost regular succession of strong and weak beats, introduces the words "quietly" and "clean," which dictate the rhythm of the end of the paragraph, when the activities of the Sunday are remembered, to the accompaniment of the discreet vibrations of "in the overlingering air." This apparently insignificant passage was chosen deliberately for the unerring sense of rhythm it shows. Faulkner's prose lives in the spoken word, and should be read aloud or in the head.

The description of Joe swallowing the dietitian's toothpaste literally ad nauseam is another passage which owes its strength to the repetitive rhythm:

> He squatted among the soft womansmelling garments and the shoes. He saw by feel alone now the ruined, once cylindrical tube. By taste and not seeing he contemplated the cool invisible worm as it coiled onto his finger and smeared sharp, automatonlike and sweet, into his mouth. By ordinary he would have taken a single mouthful and then replaced the tube and left the room. Even at five, he knew that he must not take more than that. Perhaps it was the animal warning him that more would make him sick; perhaps the human being warning him that if he took more than that, she would miss it. This was the first time he had taken more. By now, hiding and waiting, he had taken a good deal more. By feel he could see the diminishing tube. He began to sweat. Then he found that he had been sweating for some time, that for some time now he had been doing nothing else but sweating. He was not hearing anything at all now. Very likely he would not have heard a gunshot beyond the curtain. He seemed to be turned in upon himself, watching himself sweating, watching himself smear another worm of paste into his mouth which his stomach did not want. Sure enough, it refused to go down. Motionless now, utterly contemplative, he seemed to stoop above himself like a chemist in his laboratory, waiting. He didn't have to wait long. At once the paste which he had already swallowed lifted inside him, trying to get back out, into the air where it was cool. It was no longer sweet. In the rife, pinkwomansmelling obscurity behind the curtain he squatted, pinkfoamed, listening to his insides, waiting with astonished fatalism for what was about to happen to him. [pp. 113–14]

We actually see Joe putting the toothpaste into his mouth only twice. The words "automatonlike" and "diminishing" may well suggest that the action was repeated many times; however, the repetition is more clearly apparent in the variations played on the word "more," used five times in about as many lines, and coming after "single mouthful": the recurrence graphically translates the rising nausea. The parallel between the start of the two successive phrases ("perhaps it was the animal warning him") reinforces the effect. The rest of the paragraph is spanned by the repetition and alternation of several words: "sweating" (or "sweat"), "hearing" (or "heard"), "watching," "waiting" (or "wait"); and again by the words "smear," "worm," "sweet," which echo the beginning of the passage and lead finally to these amazing compound adjectives, "pinkwomansmelling" and "pink-foamed." They link women and nausea together in Joe's mind, or rather in his body, forever afterwards, and stamp his aversion with an unforgettable color. The passage is composed of short, simple sentences, but the reader forgets their divisions since they do not represent unities of sense or rhythm. The whole flows on in rhythmic waves which rise and fall on the repetitions. The passage also illustrates Faulkner's use of sonority. Even though it does not seem that he tried aloud what he wrote, as Flaubert did in his study at Croisset, which he used to call his "gueuloir," Faulkner, poet and word-musician that he is, must have listened carefully to his prose in the chamber of his mind. The waves of rhythm are music in themselves. Moreover, alliteration and assonance abound in the passage: "cool" is echoed in "coiled," and all the *s, th, sh,* and *tch* sounds, grouped around the words "sweating" and "watching," seem to prolong the disagreeable sensation of sweating and emphasize the imminence of disaster. The beginning of the paragraph makes greater use of the muffled *oo* sounds, and of the plaintive *e* sounds ("shoes," "ruined," "tube," "cool," "mouth," "mouthful," "room," "knew"; "feel," "seeing," "finger," "smear," "sweet"). The music is more insistent toward the middle of the paragraph, where the *e* sounds become obsessive ("By feel he could see the diminishing tube"), reinforced by the many present participles. Faulkner's mastery of rhythm and sonority could be illustrated in many other passages, where the effects are perhaps more striking or more sustained than in the two quoted above; for instance, one thinks of the passages referring to Christmas in the interminable street, or the second phase of his relationship with Joanna, or his death, or to Hightower's wheel and his final vision. Yet the selected passages are convincing in their very simplicity.

Discussing the language of Faulkner's characters, Warren Beck has said: "He has fully mastered the central difficulty, to retain verisimilitude while subjecting the prolix and monotonous raw material of most natural speech to an artistic pruning and pointing up."[5] This refinement of the dialogue is mostly achieved through the skill guiding the cadences and repetitions. In this sense the dialogues in *Light in August* are not greatly different from the narration, and have similar characteristics, as has already been remarked. Faulkner's work to this end can be seen in a comparison of the original and final versions of the conversation between Armstid and Winterbottom in chapter 1 (in each case, the passages of interspersed narration have been omitted). First, the original text (which is that of the salesman's dummy, preceding the University of Virginia manuscript; the latter, which is much closer to the final text, can also be used in this comparison: see the transcript of page 3 of the manuscript, which is reproduced in this volume):

"Who is it?" Winterbottom said . . . . "She couldn't have come very far in that shape."

"And before she goes much further, she is goin' to have company," Armstid said . . . . "Maybe she is visitin' around here somewhere."

While Henry Armstid and Winterbottom were squatting against the shady wall of Winterbottom's stable, they saw her pass in the road. They saw at once that she was young, pregnant, and a stranger. Winterbottom said, "I wonder where she got that belly at." Armstid said, "I wonder how far she has brot it afoot."

"Visiting somebody back down the road," Winterbottom said.

"I reckon not," Armstid said. "Or I would have heard. And it aint nobody up the way she is going, neither. I would have heard that too."

"I reckon she knows where she is going," Winterbottom said. "She walks like it."

"She'll have company, before she gets much further," Armstid said. The woman had gone on, slowly, with her swelling and unmistakable burden. Neither of them had seen her so much as look at them when she passed, in a ~~dress~~ shapeless garment of faded blue, carrying a palm leaf fan and a small cloth bundle. There was something about her that said plainer than words that she had come from a distance. Yet it was not fatigue. She seemed to walk in, to bear with her like an aura, a (?) affirmation that this was not the first afternoon or they the first strange faces which had seen her pass so: [pregnant,] slow, unhurried and timeless as augmenting afternoon itself. She went on.

"She must be visiting around here somewhere," Winterbottom said.

Transcript of page 3 of the manuscript. Cf. *Light in August*, pp. 6–7. The word crossed out in the transcript was struck out in the manuscript; the word in brackets was added in the margin by Faulkner; and the question mark indicates an undecipherable word.

"Maybe so," Winterbottom said, "I ain't heard tell though."

Now the final version (p. 7):

"I wonder where she got that belly," Winterbottom said.

"I wonder how far she has brought it afoot," Armstid said.

"Visiting somebody back down the road, I reckon," Winterbottom said.

"I reckon not. Or I would have heard. And it aint nobody up my way, neither. I would have heard that, too."

"I reckon she knows where she is going," Winterbottom said. "She walks like it."

"She'll have company, before she goes much further," Armstid said. . . . "She aint come from nowhere close . . . . She's hitting that lick like she's been at it for a right smart while and had a right smart piece to go yet."

"She must be visiting around here somewhere," Winterbottom said.

"I reckon I would have heard about it," Armstid said.

The second version does not add any information to the first: the substance is the same in each. The differences are only revealing of Faulkner's art, for which reason they are full of interest. To begin with, the author has replaced the abstract word "shape" with the more concrete "belly," which acquires its full weight with Armstid's remark: "I wonder how far she has brought it afoot." The dialogue now has the true flavor of actual speech, which the original version lacked, because of the sonorous and picturesque expression "hitting that lick," and because of the Southern farmer turns of phrase ("right smart while," echoed in "right smart piece"; these three expressions do not yet appear in the manuscript). Originally, Faulkner was satisfied with one detail of pronunciation (dropping the final "g" of the present participle), which is too common a trait to signify any one regional dialect. He has also concretized more fully the locality: "around here somewhere" is vague and does not suggest any actual place, nor does it suit the conversation of men who know their area and calculate directions in relation to their own farms; the phrases "back

down the road" and "up my way" are more typical. (He
uses "visiting around here somewhere" later on, when
vagueness becomes necessary after the remark: "She aint
come from nowhere close.") Such little details individualize
the two men: although they are only minor characters,
seen only in this first chapter, they are brought to life
through the precision of this truly spoken conversation
better than they could have been in a long description.
They are clearly Southern farmers living in a specific region.

The dialogue is also striking for its cadences. Apart
from the repetition of "maybe," the original version has
none of the echoes which give the final version its internal
rhythm: "I wonder" comes twice, "I reckon" is used three
times, and again at the end (in fact, the first "I reckon"
was not yet introduced in the manuscript following the
first known text, that of the salesman's dummy); "visiting"
recurs twice, "I would have heard" three times. The repetitions give the dialogue the rhythm of speech, unite its
various elements, and, most of all, slow it down, thus altering
its artistic significance. By the repetitions, the author represents in the text itself the slow ways of these men squatting
beneath the shady wall of a barn, not to be hurried by
anything. Thus, the passage does not only give some information about Lena, it also gives the insignia of these
farmers, who are characterized by the "timeless unhaste
and indirection of [their] kind." The alterations and additions demonstrate Faulkner's perfect mastery of dialogue.

IMAGERY

As we have already seen, certain words or images are
so persistent that they eventually become the symbols of
the characters they describe: Brown is represented as an
animal, Christmas as a shadow, and Hightower as always
bathed in sweat. Little can be gained by examining them
further. It is more rewarding to look at some of the
significant images running through the book and tightening

its texture. The images connected with sexuality are particularly worthy of note. All that is needed here is the coordination and elaboration of what has already been outlined, especially in the study of the themes of the novel. Everything which has to do with sexuality and femininity is warm, moist, dark, and thick, and is strikingly evoked in the image of the well or the pit. At the age of fourteen Christmas stands on the brink: "he seemed to look down into a black well and at the bottom saw two glints like reflection of dead stars" (p. 147). Later on he sees himself in his affair with Joanna as "a man being sucked down into a bottomless morass" (p. 246), and shortly before he kills her he feels oppressed, as though he were right at the bottom: "As from the bottom of a thick black pit he saw himself enclosed . . ." (p. 107). These unwholesome depths are peopled with monsters (octopus and Medusa), and constitute a dark domain of impurity and filth. Hence the many images of thick dark water and of liquid putrefaction: "a whispering of gutter filth," "a thick still black pool of more than water" (p. 99; cf. p. 246); "periodical filth" (p. 173); "it was as though he had fallen into a sewer" (p. 242); "living not alone in sin but in filth" (p. 244); "something liquid, deathcolored, and foul" (p. 178); "that rotten richness ready to flow into putrefaction at a touch, like something growing in a swamp" (pp. 247–48).

There are two opposites to this formless, treacherous abyss. The first is the straight, cool street, which has a clear-cut, masculine form. When Joe feels himself being dragged downward he clings to the idea of the street:

> What he was now seeing was the street lonely, savage, and cool. That was it: cool; he was thinking, saying aloud to himself sometimes, "I better move. I better get away from here." [p. 246]

The second opposite is the hill: Joe escapes from Freedman Town by climbing up the hill, and is only restored to calmness when he reaches the top and breathes the "cold hard air of white people" (p. 107); he dare not look back until he has reached the very top, the exact opposite of the abyss: "he did not look back until he reached the crest of the hill"(p. 108). So the qualities of the male world are the contrasting ones to those of the female world. This male world is frequently characterized by the word "hard"; it is pure, cool, or even cold; its waters are clean and refreshing and as light as dew. Once he has removed the last button from his underclothes, Joe sees no more images of the thick corrupted water which previously filled his mind: instead, symbolically naked, he feels the purifying cool air on his body: "he could feel the dark air like water; he could feel the dew under his feet as he had never felt dew before" (p. 100). After two hours' sleep in the stables, another symbol of virility, he goes outside and breathes in the "clean chill" of the air at dawn (p. 102), feels the grass blades against his legs like "strokes of limber icicles." Then he shaves himself, using the clean waters of a spring for a mirror. When at the age of fourteen he had refused the Negro girl, he had felt the brush upon his body of a still lighter element, a purifing wind: "There was no She at all now. They just fought; it was as if a wind had blown among them, hard and clean" (p. 147).

Throughout this novel, copulation and brutality are inseparable; it is all at once a struggle, a rape, and a robbery: "Even after a year it was as though he entered by stealth to despoil her virginity each time anew" (p. 221). The theme of sexuality is thus equally associated with all the striking images of strife and defeat which characterize Joe's relationship with Joanna: "to struggle," "physical combat," "enemy," "resistance," "surrender," "capitulation," "a defeated general on the day after the last battle" (chapters 11 and 12).

Even more striking are the frequent references to death in connection with sexuality. The eyes of the Negro girl

are "two glints like reflection of dead stars"; Bobbie's are
depthless and reflectionless, her motionless hands look "as
big and dead and pale as a piece of cooking meat," and
she has "a dead mouth in a dead face" (pp. 202 and
204). In Christmas's vision the foul liquid pouring from
the cracked urns is "deathcolored"; and when he takes
Joanna brutally for the second time, she is like a corpse
(the necrophilia of "A Rose for Emily" is brought forcibly
to mind): "beneath his hands the body might have been
the body of a dead woman not yet stiffened" (p. 223). At
a later stage, he feels as though each night were the last
under the last moon, and by day Joanna seems to be "a
phantom of someone whom the night sister had murdered
and which now moved purposeless about the scenes of
old peace, robbed even of the power of lamenting" (p.
248). This is yet another image with strong Shakespearian
overtones.

The relationship of Joe and Joanna follows the rhythm
of the seasons, but it is significant that at no time does
it evoke a beginning, a dawn, or a spring, and there are
no images of happy fertility: "During the first phase it
had been as though he were outside a house where snow
was on the ground, trying to get into the house; during
the second phase he was at the bottom of a pit in the
hot wild darkness; now he was in the middle of a plain
where there was no house, not even snow, not even wind"
(pp. 254-55). Their passion (if such it may be called) is
set in a wasteland, the desert of love. We do not know
for certain when Joe raped Joanna but it is certain that
their relationship itself has no spring, beginning in September: "It was summer becoming fall, with already, like
shadows before a westering sun, the chill and implacable
import of autumn cast ahead upon summer; something
of dying summer spurting again like a dying coal, in the
fall. This was over a period of two years" (p. 247); and
again: "that final upflare of stubborn and dying summer

upon which autumn, the dawning of halfdeath, had come unawares" (p. 251). Joanna's menopause coincides with the first frost, and when, manlike once more, she sends for Joe, it is February (pp. 252-53). Thus the changing seasons not only describe their relationship through a series of metaphors and similes, but they also become its appropriate background, its obsessive obbligato. Lena too, as will be remembered, is characterized in similar terms: she has the unhaste of a change of season, but since she belongs to immemorial earth and is eternal Nature, she contains their passage without being their slave. Images drawn from nature then are applied with contrasting significance to the two characters embodying two opposed concepts of Woman. This type of imagery helps to distinguish between the two aspects of one theme, and to bring two characters close enough for their differences to be the more obvious. A further result is that the unity of the work is cemented beyond the level of the plots themselves.

The unifying function of opposing and complementary images can be seen even more clearly in the use of the straight line and the circle. Richard Chase sees them as the central images around which *Light in August* was built, and finds them more important than the contrast of light and shadow embodied in Lena and Joe.[6] Joe's life has the rectilinear, masculine form suggested by the images of the street and the corridor. (On one occasion, he is himself compared to a lonely telephone pole in the middle of a desert.) He is associated with the street the first time the reader sees him, and on the last morning before he kills Joanna, the day itself seems like a corridor: "he could see the yellow day opening peacefully on before him like a corridor . . ." (p. 104). The image is discreetly insistent throughout the rest of the chapter: he reads his magazine straight through, "like a man walking along a street might count the cracks in the pavement, to the last and final page, the last and final word" (p. 104), and he spends the morning in a peaceful valley. This pastoral avatar of the street has a dual significance: the tranquillity it suggests could either be a prefiguration of the tranquillity he experiences eight days later, or an ironic inversion of his actual state of mind, for his street is also a prison, and he must follow it to the bitter end, "to the last and final page, the last and final word." This idea is even more pronounced in the next chapter when the first image entering his memory is that of a corridor: the orphanage is, in his mind, a long, cold, deserted corridor from which the child could no more escape than could an animal from the zoo or a criminal from a penitentiary. Then the image of the street becomes the central motif of chapter 10, leading Joe straight to Joanna's house—and finally to Mottstown, the end of his enforced journey. Joanna's house is only one more stop along the way: it is synonymous with the abyss, or the womb, and totally opposite to the street, so that, although he cannot escape from it for three years, Joe knows that it is not his true element and that he will have to leave. From the darkness of Miss Burden's kitchen he seems to stare into the street, which is the place where he must live: "the savage and lonely street which he had chosen of his own will, waiting for him, thinking *This is not my life. I dont belong here*" (pp. 243-44; cf. pp. 250-51).

Lena, the complete and self-sufficient being, is associated with the circle, a symbol of plenitude and eternity. It appears in the wheels of the wagons in which she travels, "a succession of creakwheeled . . . avatars" (p. 6), in the Keatsian urn around whose sides she moves without progress, in the circular form of the novel which she opens and closes, and even in her body, rounded by pregnancy. Yet Lena is also associated with the straight line of the road and continuous travel. She sets off from Alabama, crosses Mississippi, and the story ends as she enters Tennessee. For her, too, the stay at Jefferson was only a temporary, enforced halt. Faulkner even uses the corridor image for her: "Behind her the four weeks, the evocation of *far*, is a peaceful corridor . . ." (p. 4). Similarly, the life of Percy Grimm, Christmas's complementary double, is associated with the same image: "He could now see his life opening before him, uncomplex and inescapable as a barren corridor . . ." (p. 426). Miss Burden's life too is bounded by the walls of a prisonlike tunnel: "She seemed to see her whole past life, the starved years, like a gray tunnel, at the far and irrevocable end of which, as unfading as a reproach, her naked breast . . . ached as though in agony . . ." (p. 250).

Conversely, the image of the circle is associated with Christmas too, ever since the dietitian offered him the round dollar and so threatened his integrity when he was five. His street eventually curves around on itself to make an imprisoning circle. While Lena's road is always open, crossing the countryside, Christmas, in all his long years of wandering, is always symbolically in a street, a closed-in space, bounded by high walls. The image evoked by the succession of his days is significant: "it seems to him now that for thirty years he has lived inside an orderly parade of named and numbered days like fence pickets . . ." (pp. 313–314). When he enters Mottstown a few days later, he understands the true significance of his imprisoning street: "It had made a circle and he is still inside of it. . . . 'But I have never got outside that circle. I have never broken out of the ring of what I have already done and cannot ever undo' " (p. 321). In contrast to Lena's circle, a sign of plenitude and of the natural cycles, Joe's is that of fatality. Hightower's life, too, is in the form of a circle, that of self-centeredness and alienation from the rest of humanity, that of his ivory tower. So the wheel of his vision is an appropriate image for the revolution, in the physical sense of the word, that completes his experience in the novel. That wheel is the wheel of torture, for he is wounded and his sweat no longer suggests tears, but blood (p. 464); it is also the wheel of thought which finally runs free, liberated by his painful confession from the braking weight of a dead life; the wheel then becomes a glowing halo, the August light by which Hightower sees, in an ecstatic instant, the whole of the humanity to which he now firmly belongs. Finally, the circle is found again in the image of the urn, which is associated with Lena, and also with Christmas and Hightower, as has already been shown.

This survey of the complementary images of the straight line and the circle shows how the same symbols are associated with different themes and characters, sometimes to point out their differences, and sometimes to highlight their similarities. Running all through the novel as they do, they suggest that it may be read at a level which reaches further than the facts themselves. Thus they are important factors in the architecture and unity of the book.

So far only a few images, and those the most noteworthy, have been discussed, but there are so many that it would be impossible to mention them all. In fact, at some points, Faulkner's whole universe becomes an image, the *expression* of his mental vision, thanks to a proliferation of metaphors and similes: "as if," "as though," "like," "it seemed" punctuate every sentence at such moments. One example is sufficient illustration: the second phase of the relationship between Joe and Joanna, at the beginning of chapter 12. The tone is set in the first short paragraph, containing four lengthening similes which make up the whole of it. Faulkner has obviously abandoned objective description to draw the reader into a world of images, subjective approximations to his vision, and the only world, the only reality he offers. The beginning of the second paragraph settles the reader inside the metaphor: "The sewer ran only by night." The following pages seem to describe real places and actual situations, but one remains inside the imaginary world created at the start of the chapter. Evoking the corruptive influence of

Joanna, a malevolent power in the form of two creatures in a single body, Faulkner once more uses similes, but *inside* the metaphorical frame already established: "like two moongleamed shapes," "like locked sisters" (p. 246). It is noticeable that in these pages Faulkner feels compelled to show this imaginary world's distance from the real world by referring as though in contrast to "real" sensations (the italics are not Faulkner's): "that surrender terrific and hard, like the breaking down of a spiritual skeleton the very sound of whose snapping fibers could be *heard* almost *by the physical ear*" (p. 242); "he thought of that other personality that seemed to exist somewhere *in physical darkness itself*" (p. 248). Faulkner's world here is in no way the objective reproduction of an actual situation: it is rather the projection, through images, of the author's emotional reactions to a situation which has no actuality whatsoever outside the realm of the imagination. The author has absolute control over the entrance to this world as he has almost completely isolated it from an objective reality. In this way he can manipulate the reader's emotions as he wishes, making him share the full intensity of his own. The images are neither for decoration nor enrichment: they are the very texture of this world which has no existence other than Faulkner's imagining.

This is an expressionist rather than an impressionist technique. Impressionism is realism pushed to extremes, a desire to imitate the inimitable and to capture evanescence, like the Seine at Les Andelys or Reims cathedral swathed in a unique and insubstantial veil of mist. Expressionism, on the other hand, seeks not to fix the quality of a given instant, not to make "a moment's monument," but to reconstruct from the artist's own reactions and the elements of his vision, a coherent reality which does not show fleeting appearances but the essential qualities, as he has glimpsed them beyond and through these appearances. The results may appear disturbingly idiosyncratic insofar as the work is the outcome of an inner compulsion working with elements which may well have been distorted in passing through the prism of a personality. James Burnham made this point as early as January 1931, in a penetrating article which has been strangely omitted from bibliographies concerning Faulkner: "Faulkner is using the data of observation only as a material in the construction of his own world. It is to be judged not as imitation but as creation, by the emotional integrity with which it is formed."[7] In a review of *Absalom, Absalom!*, Clifton Fadiman noted: "Very few things in the book remain themselves. Each one reminds Mr. Faulkner of something else."[8] The critic of *The New Yorker* meant thus to censure an author he steadily refused to understand, but he has accurately described an art which seeks less to describe an external reality than to re-create an inner vision in language which will provoke a similar vision in the reader's mind. The constant use of similes, the series of approximations, the translation of emotions into images (techniques which Fadiman calls the memory of something else) are the methods Faulkner uses to woo the reader into a state of empathy so that he may share the author's vision. Like all expressionist art, Faulkner's bears the marks of the violence inferred in the projection, the *ex-pression*, of an inner vision. Just as Soutine's *Rooster* seems torn, lynched as it were, or as the colors in a Rouault or a Kokoschka seem to scream out, or as Van Gogh's yellows are thrust onto the canvas with a sort of frenzy, so Faulkner translates his vision into a language that can be scorchingly intense, and loads an emotion-releasing prose with his own (occasionally discordant) reactions toward a character or a landscape.

Faulkner's style in *Light in August* has a remarkable unity of tone. The characteristics we have defined are present all the time at all levels of the writing. Both dialogues and characters' narrations, although written in a truly spoken language, are as rich in images and rhythms as the passages presented in the author's own voice. Moreover, as has already been mentioned, Faulkner has great skill in amplifying and *augmenting* voices so that the differences between his characters' and his own are smoothed away, leaving the unity unimpaired. This does not mean though that Faulkner's style has no variety. He subtly modulates his prose to fit each character. Lena's calm endurance, for instance, is suggested in the regular rhythms and by the recurrence of words which quickly become musical motifs, giving the prose a richness and consistence characteristic of the woman herself. When he describes a wagon hypnotically suspended in the Southern light, the style becomes that of poetry. For Hightower, the style is more ornate, more complex, even precious and self-conscieous, self-centered as befits the character. Chapter 3 in particular offers examples of this, in the studied inversions ("by bushing crape myrtle and syringa and Althea almost hidden," p. 52), chiasmus ("the sign, carpentered neatly by himself and by himself lettered," p. 53), and of preciosity in the use of words and sonorities ("that instant when all light has failed out of the sky and it would be night save for that faint light which daygranaried leaf and grass blade reluctant suspire, making still a little light on earth though night itself has come," p. 55). The minister's incoherence in his sermons is mirrored in Faulkner's deliberate anacoluthon:

> up there in the pulpit with his hands flying around him and the dogma he was supposed to preach all full of galloping cavalry and defeat and glory . . ., it in turn would get all mixed up with absolution and choirs of martial seraphim, until it was natural that the old men and women should believe that what he preached . . . verged on actual sacrilege. [p. 57]

Finally, images and rhythms are exploited to their full effect in the account of Christmas's life, in some of the finest passages that Faulkner ever wrote. In fact, these six chapters are unforgettable, and they have provided most of the illustrations for this study of his style. They never sink into the moralizing rhetoric which occasionally can become unbearable in a few of the later novels, whose significance at times seems obscured rather than enriched by such mannerisms. The grandeur of *Light in August* has its source not only in its subtle structure, the forceful presence of its characters, and the wealth and variety of its themes, but also in the mastery of its style, a style in which a poetic sense of rhythm and sound, a powerful imagination and a steady control of technique remain firmly harnessed to the author's purposes. The remarkable mastery of language places *Light in August* alongside Faulkner's greatest masterpieces.

7

Reception
and Interpretations

IT HAS ALREADY BEEN SAID that on the publication of *Light in August* and in the following years, the true dimension of the work was often not fully appreciated. *Sanctuary* had shocked many people and for some time Faulkner was classed among those authors who use sex and violence to boost their sales. He seemed then to be one of the leaders of the so-called school of cruelty.[1] (It is interesting to speculate on whether Faulkner's reputation would have been different during these years if, in 1932, instead of *Sanctuary,* Random House had published *Light in August* in a Modern Library edition—thus making it known to a much wider reading public.) However, in spite of dissatisfaction with that raw depiction of life, and with the plot structure and the role of Hightower, one must acknowledge that a fair proportion of the reviewers were by no means unfavorable to the novel, but instead found the author's Gothic romanticism unusually impressive, and praised his remarkable vigor and mastery. Around the forties, Marxist criticism ostracized Faulkner because he had no social conscience and could not perceive the distant dawning of a brave new world. The result was that *Light in August,* like so many other of Faulkner's novels, had to wait until the fifties for general recognition of its real significance. Indeed, it seems that this novel had for some time been denied the awed attention offered to other more difficult or more obscure masterpieces, to the extent that, with a few brilliant exceptions, most of the serious critical studies of the work only date from the last ten or fifteen years.

However, judging by the number of translations, *Light in August* is one of Faulkner's most widely read novels abroad. Allowing for error in a matter so difficult to assess, the novel has been translated into sixteen languages, on a par with *The Sound and the Fury, Intruder in the Dust,* and *The Wild Palms (Sanctuary* and *The Unvanquished* can be read in thirteen different languages, and *As I Lay Dying* in twelve). If one takes 1946 (the year of publication of Malcolm Cowley's *The Portable Faulkner),* or better still 1950 (the award of the Nobel Prize), as the beginning of Faulkner's fame with the general public and even among critics, it is remarkable that *Light in August* heads the field among the novels translated before 1950. After *Intruder in the Dust* and *The Wild Palms* it is also the most widely translated of his novels in the socialist or communist countries.

In France Faulkner's reputation was established very early as a result of the attention paid him by Malraux, Valéry Larbaud, Sartre, and, most of all, by his best translator and interpreter to the French public, Maurice E. Coindreau, who translated *As I Lay Dying* as early as 1934, *Light in August* in 1935, and *The Sound and the Fury* in 1938, plus a good number of Faulkner's best short stories.

The more than two hundred reviews, articles, chapters, or brief passages which have been devoted to *Light in August* are far from unanimous in their interpretations of the novel. The preceding pages have already suggested that it could be understood in different ways, because of the ambiguities and obscurities which are present in the themes and the characters alike. The subtle complexity of

Faulkner's technique does not simplify the matter since it creates a mirror play between the characters, who reflect from one to another images which are both similar and inverted, and an echo play which sets up endless sympathetic vibrations in many deeds, gestures, words, and thoughts. It is therefore useless to spend very long on the matter: a brief look at the various opinions, grouped under general headings, with some elaboration in places, will suffice. For the sake of simplicity we will divide the interpretations into four sections: Gothic, existential, mythological, and humanist.

GOTHIC INTERPRETATIONS

The critical history of *Light in August* shows that the major part of the Gothic interpretations were put forward when the book was first published. Miss Burden's sombre house, the nightmarish quality of Joe's life during his relationship with Joanna, the macabre scenes, the violence and the sadism, the apparent Manichaeism suggested by the juxtaposition of the worlds of Lena and Joe, of light and shadow, and by the confrontation between the two in Joe's conscience and flesh—all these explain why *Light in August* has often been classed with *Sanctuary* as a gruesome story. The title of one of the first reviews, "Nigger in a Woodpile," sums up the attitude: "Not nearly so horrible as *Sanctuary*," writes its anonymous author, "it would still make hair-raising cinema of the *Dr. Caligari* model. . . . *Light in August* continues the Faulkner tradition by a murder, a lynching and a good deal of morbid fornication."[2] Herschel Brickell agrees: "Mr. Faulkner has turned his consummate skill to the creation of a South that exists only in his fiery and tortured imagination . . . he is really writing Gothic romances in the modernistic manner."[3] In France, Charles Cestre's brief study shows a similar attitude: he sees the novel as bathed in madness and nightmare, and aptly typified by the author's style, "tropical forests where splendid thickets rise at every step one takes," a description which is perhaps true of later works, but not of *Light in August*.[4] The Gothic horror and violence have so struck some critics that they have construed it as an end in itself, not a means to an end: "Mr. Faulkner is a thorough romantic," writes Geoffrey Stone in *The Bookman*. "It is evident in his love of violence for its own sake and the pretentiousness with which he loads every paragraph. . . . The book seems at times like an epileptic fit, a fierce straining against nothing."[5] A month later the same *Bookman* recommended the novel in a list of Christmas gifts as "intellectual blood and thunder." Although one may still hear a few remarks of this nature, critical opinion as a whole finds support in Faulkner's own comments for the conviction that the Gothic atmosphere is nothing more than a tool the author found at hand. However, it is true that there exists a permanent Gothic strain in the Southern novel, witness the work of Flannery O'Connor or Truman Capote, or the more recent *Deliverance*, by James Dickey.

MYTHOLOGICAL INTERPRETATIONS

Mythological interpretations were undoubtedly encouraged by the rediscovery of the ancient myths, especially after the one-volume publication of *The Golden Bough* in 1922, and they were justified by the deliberate use of myths by such writers as Joyce and T. S. Eliot. The latter describes the "mythical method" in his essay "Ulysses, Order and Myth": "In using the myth, in manipulating a continuous parallel between contemporaneity and antiquity, Mr. Joyce is pursuing a method which others must pursue after him. . . . Psychology . . . ethnology and *The Golden Bough* have concurred to make possible what was impossible even a few years ago. Instead of narrative method, we may now use the mythical method."[6] Although Faulkner told Henry Nash Smith in 1932 that he had never read *Ulysses*,[7] it appears likely that he read at least some extracts when the novel was published in serial form in *The Little Review,* between March 1918 and December 1920, or such is the opinion of Richard P. Adams.[8] *The Little Review* was in fact one of those influential literary periodicals to which his friend Phil Stone subscribed (he also took *The Dial,* where Faulkner may have read Eliot's essay on *Ulysses*). Whatever the truth of this, mythological references quickly appeared in his work, their importance culminating in *A Fable.* Consequently, some critics have felt it legitimate to establish strict parallels between *Light in August* and some myth or other. These interpretations, it is true, throw new light on the characters, but they may also deform them in re-creating them to fulfill the demands of a limited concept. To avoid repetition, we will not mention further the Christian myths, but restrict ourselves to discussion of one or two original, if at times tenuous, interpretations.

The most stimulating of these is Beach Langston's: "Lena Grove and Hightower are incarnate manifestations of the fertility goddess Diana of the Grove of Nemi and of the recurring figure of Buddha, or more accurately, of a Bodhisattva."[9] Langston finds explicit resemblances between Lena and Diana as described in *The Golden Bough,* expecially in the first chapter of the one-volume edition: "Both are nature and fertility goddesses; both are huntresses (though Lena's quarry is a husband); though unmarried both have childbirth as their particular concern; and both are associated with fire in August.[10] Byron Bunch has to fight Lucas Burch before replacing him as Lena's lover, just as an aspirant to the priesthood of Diana had to vanquish the incumbent before he could become the local Jupiter and mate with Diana of the Grove." The parallels are of definite interest, but the question remains: is it necessary to identify Lena precisely with Diana of Nemi? There is nothing to support it in Faulkner's text: he has explained that for him Lena Grove evoked pagan antiquity and not any one particular mother goddess. Langston's desire to prove the legitimacy of his parallel here leads to interpretations too far fetched to be credible.

His ideas on Hightower are of greater interest and originality. The comparison of Hightower with an eastern idol and the recurrence of the word "avatar" in the novel (though not applied to this character) encourage Langston to note that Hightower, like Buddha's disciples, has two possible roads to salvation: the lesser, Hinayana, is the way of passivity and retreat, and the greater, Mahayana, is that which follows enlightenment. According to Langston, the end of chapter 16 shows Hightower's renunciation of the first path, that of nirvana: his flesh seems to fall away and disintegrate as he lies prone on his desk, his arms extended, in an attitude of rejection of the past and acceptance of life. The living sound of insects does not falter or cease, and in the next chapter, Hightower rises and delivers Lena's child. Langston explains:

> In terms of the Buddha parallel, these two chapters mean that Hightower has died to or rejected the earlier, negativistic, ascetic concept of nirvana as withdrawal from this physical world and is now ready for that kind of enlightenment which came to Buddha under the Bo-tree at the Deer Park in Benares, where he first set in motion the Wheel of the Law. Essentially this enlightenment consists in the acceptance of *pari-nirvana,* that infinite and eternal peace into which the enlightened Bodhisattva may enter when he has worked out his karma and thus broken the chain of reincarnation.

In view of this, the image of the wheel, as a sign that the soul has completed the circle of its existence and has no further need of reincarnation, would be appropriate to Hightower. The "now. Now" which ushers in his vision at the end of chapter 20 would mark this entrance into *pari-nirvana.* However, this brilliant interpretation of Hightower errs in trying to establish too strict a parallel between a character and any given myth. There is nothing to suggest that Hightower enters his nirvana at the end, and the violent images of the cavalry have no relation to the promised peace. Faulkner wished above all, or such is the contention of this study, to show Hightower's painful return to life, responsibility, and solidarity, and he has explained that Hightower would have to go on living and enduring.[11] Finally, Faulkner stated in an excellent interview in 1952 his ignorance of the Hindu world: "I don't know India, and know nothing about oriental civilizations—it's one of my gaps."[12] How far he is to be believed is another matter.

Another interesting interpretation comes from Robert M. Slabey, but he tries too hard to fit *Light in August* into the mythical structures suggested by Sir James Frazer:

> Joe Christmas is not a "Christ" figure but a *Golden Bough* figure. The events of his life story and the imagery with which they are told are related to an archetypal experience. *Light in August* is part of an "eternal" framework: the journey of the classical hero in his mythological descent into the abyss and meeting with the Shadow (the Shadow which is his own "dark" side); the timeless sequence of withdrawal and return, death and rebirth, analogous to the principle of organic growth, a rhythmic experience close to the heart of Man, recorded in art and literature from prehistoric time to "atomic" time.[13]

So Slabey finds parallels between the life of Joe Christmas and the myth of Adonis, suggests the double face of Aphrodite in Joanna's dual personality ("the two creatures . . . in the one body . . . locked like sisters," p. 246), and sees Joe's renaissance in the birth of Lena's child and, even more, in the spiritual experience of this man who has plunged into the Negro world (Hell, death) and then emerged to find peace in the dawn of a Friday morning. Such a reading of *Light in August* as a death and rebirth myth would throw new light on chapter 14, but would hardly correspond with the overall impression of Joe's life. It has the same fault as all the other interpretations: in trying to prove itself, it loses sight of some of the author's intentions, and further, like its fellows, it is too narrow to allow for the ambiguities and indecisions of the work and so limits its total significance.

The last two groups do not require a lengthy investigation here. In another article, Robert M. Slabey refers to Camus, Sartre, and Heidegger in his efforts to make Christmas into an existentialist hero.[14] Indeed, it is true that Christmas has much in common with "the stranger" of Camus or Kafka, who is confronted with an absurd world, which denies his identity and even his existence. Yet the parallel is a little superficial: Faulkner's world does not so much suggest that of Kafka or Sartre as that of Hawthorne in that it is haunted by puritanism and riddled with evil. If there is a similarity to Sartre, it lies rather in the conception of the look expressing possessive relationships between people, as has been noted in the study of the characters. In fact, Sartre refers to *Light in August* in this context to illustrate how sadism holds the seeds of its own failure:

> The sadist discovers his error when his victim *looks* at him; that is, when the sadist experiences the absolute alienation of his being in the Other's freedom. . . . He discovers then that he cannot act on the Other's freedom even by forcing the Other to humiliate himself and to beg for mercy, for it is precisely in and through the Other's absolute freedom that there exists a world in which there is sadism and instruments of torture and a hundred pretexts for being humiliated and for forswearing oneself. Nobody has better portrayed the power of the victim's look at his torturers than Faulkner has done in the final pages of *Light in August*.[15]

In the same spirit, William J. Sowder persists in seeing Christmas as a brother of Roquentin *(Nausea):*[16] they are both, he says, "victims of existential rape," and both experience nausea for the same reasons: "Realizing that they were wholly unnecessary to their worlds they were victims of existential anguish." Yet Sowder's own excessive devotion to this theory demolishes it for he eventually completely deforms Faulkner's character:

> Christmas, like Roquentin, . . . was not a sexual cripple victimized by unconscious drives which he did not understand; rather, he abhorred sexuality because it served a base and useless purpose; the sexual act made life possible, and life, as the dietitian and McEachern had proved to him, was superfluous, futile, filthy. People were to him what they were to Garcin, the Object-hero of No-Exit—"hell." Even though Christmas knew that Miss Burden was at her age unlikely to have a child, the thought of being responsible for another unnecessary excrescence upon a wholly meaningless universe was too heavy for him to bear, and he killed her.

Faulkner suggests nothing of the sort.

It is needless to return to the humanist interpretation which sees the novel as an allegory of the human condition, an illustration through Joe, Lena, and Hightower of the ways by which a man may affirm his existence: he may choose revolt and solitude, both sterile and deadly, yet consonant with human dignity, or he may choose acceptance, responsibility, and solidarity. This is in fact the most generally held conception of the novel, and the one to which this study runs closest. Faulkner himself, in reply to a Japanese who asked him to which school he adhered, said that he belonged to none, and added: "I would say, . . . the only school I belong to, that I want to belong to, is the humanist school." [17]

Notes

UNLESS OTHERWISE STATED, references to other works of Faulkner's are to the Random House editions, which have the same pagination as the originals, and are sometimes photographic reproductions of them.

Frequent references are also made to the following works:

Faulkner in the University: Class Conferences at the University of Virginia 1957-1958, ed. Frederick L. Gwynn and Joseph L. Blotner (Charlottesville: University of Virginia Press, 1959; New York: Vintage Books, 1965). Abbreviated to *FU.*

Essays, Speeches and Public Letters by William Faulkner, ed. James B. Meriwether (New York: Random House, 1965). Abbreviated to *ESPL.*

Lion in the Garden: Interviews with William Faulkner, 1926-1962, ed. James B. Meriwether and Michael Millgate (New York: Random House, 1968). Abbreviated to *LG.*

When the references are incomplete in the notes, they will be found in full in the Selected and Critical Bibliography at the end of the book.

1. OVERVIEW AND COMPOSITION

1. See the beginning of chap. 7.

2. *FU,* pp. 49-50. Cf. his reply to a question from Jean Stein about his obsession with violence: "That's like saying the carpenter is obsessed with his hammer. Violence is simply one of the

carpenter's tools. The writer can no more build with one tool than the carpenter can" (*LG*, p. 248). As early as 1935, in the preface to his translation of *Light in August*, Maurice E. Coindreau wrote, very aptly: "William Faulkner, no matter what some have said about him, does not use horror gratuitously. His work has a quality of inevitability; and it is not with steady nerves that one should approach it but with an intellect prepared to exert itself. . . ." (*The Time of William Faulkner: A French View of Modern American Fiction,* edited and translated by George McMillan Reeves, Columbia: University of South Carolina Press, 1971, p. 32. The French text is in Coindreau's preface, Paris: Gallimard, 1935, p. VIII.)

3. *LG*, p. 255.

4. *LG*, p. 248.

5. See John B. Cullen, with Floyd D. Watkins, *Old Times in the Faulkner Country,* chap. XII: "Joe Christmas and Nelse Patton."

6. Ibid., p. 63.

7. Louis D. Rubin, Jr., "Notes on a Rear-Guard Action," p. 36. Some of the misreadings already mentioned seem to make their way into the comments of this distinguished critic. Cleanth Brooks disposes once and for all of the assumption that Christmas is lynched (*William Faulkner,* pp. 51-52 and 377; see bibliog. chap. 2).

8. Malcolm Cowley, *The Portable Faulkner* (New York: The Viking Press, 1946), p. 652. This interpretation remains unchanged in the revised and expanded edition (1967, p. 584).

9. *FU*, p. 265.

10. *FU*, p. 199. See below, in chap. 3, "Characters and Myths."

11. Irving Howe, *William Faulkner*, p. 209 (see bibliog. chap. 2).

12. Richard P. Adams, *Faulkner: Myth and Motion*, p. 84 (see bibliog. chap. 2).

13. *LG*, p. 23.

14. This letter is now part of the Linton Massey collection in the Alderman Library at the University of Virginia. Reproduction is temporarily forbidden.

15. This text is in fact the introduction to a limited edition of *The Sound and the Fury* intended for publication by Random House in 1933, for which Faulkner once thought of using colored inks, had publishing been advanced enough, to indicate thought transferences in Benjy's section. Written after the publication of *Light in August,* this important introduction is also a review of

the author's literary career so far, an assertion of his self-confidence in his "trade," and a profession of his dedication to his art. Faulkner worked on the text carefully, almost as though on a poem, as he wrote in another letter to Ben Wasson, reproduction of which is also temporarily forbidden. The four-page typescript (the first page is missing) is in the Faulkner collection at the University of Virginia. It is for the most part unpublished, except for the passages quoted by Michael Millgate in *The Achievement of William Faulkner,* pp. 26, 33-34 and 132.

2. Structure and Technique

1. See chap. 3, "The Voice."

2. See below, remarks on chap. 19, and, in chap. 3 of this study, "The Ambiguity of the Characters."

3. Richard Chase, "The Stone and the Crucifixion: Faulkner's *Light in August,*" *The Kenyon Review,* 10 (Autumn 1948), pp. 539-51. Elmo Howell, in "Reverend Hightower and the Uses of Southern Adversity," *College English,* 24 (Dec. 1962), pp. 183-87, thinks that even though his self-confession brings him peace, Hightower is still bound up in his past.

4. This is a vexed question. Ten or more critics agree that Hightower does in fact die. The parallels with the death of Christmas, as well as several of the comments just before the vision, which would in this case have been his last, support this view. He himself thinks he is dying, "it seems to him that some ultimate dammed flood within him breaks and rushes away" (p. 466), and he feels as though his body, empty and useless, is losing contact with the earth. But the last sentence of the chapter seems to contradict this with its suggestion that he still hears the cavalry after its passage. Faulkner said that Hightower did not die (see quotation later on). However, does it really matter whether he dies or not? Neither supposition affects the character's conception or the overall impression of the book, as Cleanth Brooks has said: "as far as the larger scheme of the book is concerned, it hardly matters: whether Hightower died or lived on, he had broken out of the circle in which we find him at the opening of the story" (*William Faulkner,* pp. 70-71).

5. *FU,* p. 75.

6. Richard P. Adams, *Faulkner: Myth and Motion,* p. 92.

7. Malcolm Cowley, *The Faulkner-Cowley File* (New York: The Viking Press, 1966), p. 29.

8. William Empson, *English Pastoral Poetry* (New York: W. W. Norton, 1938), p. 54. The recurrence of certain symbols and images has the same effect as repeated situations, tightening the structure of the novel through the web of echoes they set up (see chap. 6).

9. A. Bleikasten, "L'espace dans *Lumière d'août*," p. 420 (see bibliog. chap. 4).

10. John L. Longley, Jr., *The Tragic Mask* (Chapel Hill: University of North Carolina Press, 1963), p. 195.

11. James W. Linn and Houghton W. Taylor, *A Foreword to Fiction* (New York: Appleton-Century-Crofts, 1935), chap. 11.

12. Note the end of chaps. 2, 3, 17, 18.

13. Cleanth Brooks, *William Faulkner*, p. 72.

14. See above, chap. 1, p. 9.

15. *FU*, p. 45.

16. *FU*, p. 77.

17. *LG*, p. 255.

18. Cf. "yesterday today and tomorrow are Is: Indivisible: One" (*Intruder in the Dust*, p. 194).

19. Linn and Taylor, p. 155.

20. *FU*, p. 74.

21. *LG*, pp. 238 and 88.

3. THE CHARACTERS

1. Herman Melville, *Moby Dick*, chap. 28: "he looked like a man cut away from the stake, when the fire has overrunningly wasted all the limbs without consuming them." Cf. *Absalom, Absalom!*: "[Sutpen] looked like a man who had been sick . . . like a man who had been through some solitary furnace experience which was more than just a fever" (p. 32).

2. See *William Faulkner: Early Prose and Poetry*, ed. Carvel Collins (Boston: Little, Brown and Co., 1962).

3. This is the description of the equestrian statue of Jackson in New Orleans: "Andrew Jackson in childish effigy bestriding the terrific arrested plunge of his curly balanced horse . . ." (*Mosquitoes*, New York: Boni and Liveright, 1927, p. 14).

4. Faulkner obviously likes this suggestive word. Beach Langston has found seventeen examples of it in the novels from *The Sound and the Fury* to *The Mansion* ("The Meaning of Lena Grove and Gail Hightower in *Light in August*," *Boston University Studies in English*, 5 [Spring 1961], pp. 46-63).

5. *Absalom, Absalom!*, pp. 8 and 31–32.

6. W. Brylowski, *Faulkner's Olympian Laugh*, p. 84, note (see bibliog. chap. 2).

7. *FU*, p. 97.

8. Beekman W. Cottrell, "Christian Symbols in *Light in August*," *Modern Fiction Studies*, 2 (Winter 1956), pp. 207–13.

9. See chap. 7.

10. For further details, see C. H. Holman, "The Unity of Faulkner's *Light in August*."

11. *New Orleans Sketches* (New Brunswick: Rutgers University Press, 1958), p. 103.

12. *FU*, p. 199.

13. In 1956 he declared to Jean Stein: "the *Ode on a Grecian Urn* is worth any number of old ladies" (*LG*, p. 239). As early as 1925 he praised the same ode for "that beautiful awareness, so sure of its own power that it is not necessary to create the illusion of force by frenzy and motion ("Verse Old and Nascent," in *William Faulkner: Early Prose and Poetry*, p. 117).

14. This idea is developed by Norman H. Pearson, "Lena Grove."

15. *FU*, pp. 86 and 117.

16. *As I Lay Dying*, p. 48.

4. THE LANDSCAPE

1. A slightly different version of this chapter appeared in *The Mississippi Quarterly*, 23 (Summer 1970), pp. 265–72.

2. See pp. 83, 85, 208, 246, 300, etc.

3. Similarly, in *As I Lay Dying*, in a journey "uninferant of progress" (p. 101), the road *is* time: "Back running, tunnelled between the two sets of bobbing mule ears, the road vanishes beneath the wagon as though it were a ribbon and the front axle were a spool" (p. 38). It is remarkable that Faulkner should use that same image of the thread and the spool to suggest the interchangeability of time and space. The image occurs again in *As I Lay Dying*, in the climactic scene of the crossing of the flooded river, when Darl, from the wagon, looks at those on the other side: "It is as though the space between us were time: an irrevocable quality. It is as though time, no longer running straight before us in a diminishing line, now runs parallel between us like a looping string, the distance being the doubling accretion of the thread and not the interval between" (p. 139).

4. The expression "dying fall," which Faulkner uses several times in his works, may be borrowed from Orsino's opening speech in *Twelfth Night:*

If music be the food of love, play on; . . .
That strain again!—it had a dying fall.

A few other Shakesperean echoes are noted in the course of this study. A remarkable crop could be gathered from a close reading of *The Sound and the Fury,* especially Quentin's section.

5. The Themes

1. Translated by George J. Becker (New York: Stocken Books Publishers, 1958), pp. 29–30. The French text is to be found in Jean-Paul Sartre, *Réflexions sur la question juive* (Paris: Gallimard, 1954), p. 35. Mark Twain censured such "instantaneous societies" in some passages which do not admit of argument, such as "The United States of Lyncherdom," or the episode of the witch hunt in *The Mysterious Stranger,* or of course, in the famous speech of Colonel Sherburn in *The Adventures of Huckleberry Finn.* See also the obsessive evocation of the composite face of the crowd in *Intruder in the Dust.*

2. Ibid., p. 49 (French edition, p. 59).

3. *The Sound and the Fury,* p. 106.

4. See below, "Alienation and Compassion."

5. *The Wild Palms,* pp. 34 and 137–38.

6. *Sanctuary* (New York: Vintage, 1958), p. 163. Cf. this remark from Mr. Compson in *The Sound and the Fury* (p. 119): "*Women are like that they dont acquire knowledge of people we are for that they are just born with a practical fertility of suspicion that makes a crop every so often and usually right they have an affinity for evil for supplying whatever the evil lacks in itself for drawing it about them instinctively as you do bedclothing in slumber fertilising the mind for it until the evil has served its purpose whether it ever existed or no.*"

7. *Sanctuary,* pp. 148 and 216.

8. C. Brooks, *William Faulkner,* p. 57 (see bibliog. chap. 2).

9. See chap. 2 (the analysis of chap. 19 of the novel), and the end of chap. 3.

10. *FU,* p. 199.

11. This letter is reproduced in *The Princeton University Library Chronicle,* 18 (Spring 1957), plate II.

12. In *Writers in Crisis* (Boston: Houghton Mifflin, 1942), Maxwell Geismar devotes to Faulkner a chapter called "The Negro and the Female" (pp. 141-83), "these twin Furies of the Faulknerian deep southern Waste Land"(p. 169). The equation of Woman with evil in *Light in August* seems unequivocal to him.

13. Faulkner's whole career in a way represents a struggle similar to that of Christmas. Robert Penn Warren defines the bases of the work thus: "It springs from . . . a need—not a program or even an intention or a criticism of society—to struggle with the painful incoherences and paradoxes of life, . . . in order to achieve meaning; . . . the great undergirding and overarching meaning of life is in the act of trying to create meaning through struggle" (*Faulkner: A Collection of Critical Essays,* ed. Robert Penn Warren, Englewood Cliffs, N.J.: Prentice-Hall, 1966, pp. 14-15).

14. *FU,* p. 118

15. *As I Lay Dying,* pp. 164 and 165-66. Cf. Fairchild in *Mosquitoes:* "You begin to substitute words for things and deeds, like the withered cuckold husband that took the Decameron to bed with him every night, and pretty soon the thing or the deed becomes justs a kind of shadow of a certain sound you make by shaping your mouth in a certain way" (New York: Boni and Liveright, 1927, p. 210).

16. *LG,* p. 253; *FU,* pp. 74, 199.

17. *ESPL,* p. 120.

18. William Van O'Connor, "Protestantism in Yoknapatawpha County," in *Southern Renascence,* p. 168.

19. In his efforts to save a Negro, Byron reminds one of Hawkshaw, an employee in a Jefferson barber shop in "Dry September"—with the difference though that heavy evidence of his guilt hangs over Christmas, while the Negro, Will Mayes, is certainly innocent, even in the eyes of some of the citizens, who, however, dare not say so (Hawkshaw is the only one with the courage to go against the racist frenzy of the loudest mouthed, and he is promptly dubbed "niggerlover"). This short story, probably written less than two years before Faulkner began *Light in August,* also shows a brutal prefiguration of Percy Grimm in the person of McLendon. In another short story, "Hair," written about the same time, the main character is this same Hawkshaw, who resembles Byron in more ways than one: "A little, sandy-complected man with a face you would not remember and would not recognize again ten minutes later . . . " (*Collected Stories,* p. 137). Anyone who remembers the furniture dealer's vivid comments

on Byron could not fail to notice the similarity. Another interesting point is that the second section of "Hair" begins with this sentence: "If there had been love once, a man would have said that Hawkshaw had forgotten her" (ibid., p. 137). The second part of chapter 2 in *Light in August* begins thus: "If there had been love once, man or woman would have said that Byron Bunch had forgotten her" (p. 42). It would seem then that Faulkner wished to recreate in Byron the Hawkshaw of the stories.

6. STYLISTIC APPROACHES

1. *As I Lay Dying,* p. 163.
2. Eric Larsen, "The Barrier of Language," p. 30.
3. Karl E. Zink, "William Faulkner: Form as Experience," p. 402.
4. Walter J. Slatoff, *Quest for Failure,* p. 242 (see bibliog. chap. 3).
5. Warren Beck, "William Faulkner's Style," p. 148.
6. Richard Chase, "The Stone and the Crucifixion."
7. James Burnham, "Trying to Say," *The Symposium,* 2 (Jan. 1931), pp. 51-59.
8. Clifton Fadiman, "Faulkner, Extra-Special, Double-Distilled," *The New Yorker,* Oct. 31, 1936, pp. 62-64.

7. RECEPTION AND INTERPRETATIONS

1. See Alan Reynolds Thompson, "The Cult of Cruelty," *The Bookman,* 74 (Jan.–Feb. 1932), pp. 477-87.
2. *Time,* Oct. 17, 1932, p. 51.
3. Herschel Brickell, "The Fruits of Diversity," *Virginia Quarterly Review,* 9 (Jan. 1933), pp. 114-19.
4. Charles Cestre, "William Faulkner: *Light in August,*" *Revue anglo-américaine,* 10 (June 1933), pp. 466-67.
5. Geoffrey Stone, "Light in August," *The Bookman,* 75 (Nov. 1932), pp. 736-38.
6. T. S. Eliot, "Ulysses, Order and Myth," *The Dial,* 75 (Nov. 1923), p. 483.
7. *LG,* p. 30.
8. Richard P. Adams, "The Apprenticeship of William Faulkner," *Tulane Studies in English,* 12 (1962), 113-56, p. 139.

9. Beach Langston, "The Meaning of Lena Grove and Gail Hightower in *Light in August*," *Boston University Studies in English*, 5 (Spring 1961), pp. 46-63.

10. See James G. Frazer, *The Golden Bough*, one-volume abridged edition (New York: Macmillan, 1922), p. 3: "During [Diana's] annual festival, held on the thirteenth of August, at the hottest time of the year, her grove shone with a multitude of torches. . . . Bronze statuettes found in her precinct represent the goddess herself holding a torch. . . ."

11. Passage already quoted. See *FU*, p. 75.

12. *LG*, p. 71.

13. Robert M. Slabey, "Myth and Ritual in *Light in August*," *Texas Studies in Literature and Language*, 2 (Autumn 1960), 328-49, p. 347.

14. Robert M. Slabey, "Joe Christmas, Faulkner's Marginal Man," *Phylon*, 21 (Fall 1960), pp. 266-77.

15. Jean-Paul Sartre, *Being and Nothingness*, special abridged edition (New York: The Citadel Press, 1964), p. 381. For the French text, see *L'Etre et le Néant* (Paris: Gallimard, 1943), p. 476.

16. William J. Sowder, "Christmas as Existentialist Hero," *University Review*, 30 (June 1964), pp. 279-84.

17. *LG*, p. 141.

Selected and Critical Bibliography

GENERAL BIBLIOGRAPHY ON *LIGHT IN AUGUST*

1. CHECKLISTS (ONLY THE MORE RECENT ARE MENTIONED):

Beebe, Maurice. "Criticism of William Faulkner: A Selected Checklist." *Modern Fiction Studies,* 13 (Spring 1967), pp. 115–61 (on *Light in August,* pp. 143–46).

Bryer, Jackson R., ed. *Fifteen Modern American Authors.* Durham, N.C.: Duke University Press, 1969. The chapter on William Faulkner (pp. 175–210), by James B. Meriwether, includes one brief page on *Light in August.*

Inge, M. Thomas. "William Faulkner's *Light in August:* An Annotated Checklist of Criticism." *Resources for American Literary Study,* 1 (Spring 1971), pp. 30–57. Inge lists about 220 items, briefly annotated, and ordered chronologically in three sections: contemporary American reviews (1932–1934), books treating the novel in chapters or sections, and periodical articles (1935–1971). Apart from reviews abroad, this is an exhaustive and up-to-date bibliography, particularly useful because it lists many contemporary reviews for the first time.

2. COLLECTIONS OF CRITICAL STUDIES:

Inge, M. Thomas, ed. *The Merrill Studies in Light in August.* Columbus, Ohio: Charles E. Merrill Publishing Co., 1971. In addition to Faulkner's own commentaries on his novel, the chapter on Joe Christmas from the book by John B. Cullen

[*169*]

and Floyd C. Watkins (see bibliog. chap. 1) and five useful reviews dating from 1932–1933, the collection contains the following articles, all of which are commented on in the bibliography or the text and notes of the present study: R. Chase, "The Stone and the Crucifixion"; D. Abel, "Frozen Movement in *Light in August*"; C. H. Holman, "The Unity of Faulkner's *Light in August*"; R. M. Slabey, "Myth and Ritual in *Light in August*"; J. M. Kimmey, "The Good Earth in *Light in August*"; J. L. Longley, Jr., "Joe Christmas: The Hero in the Modern World"; B. R. McElderry, Jr., "The Narrative Structure of *Light in August*."

Minter, David L., ed. *Twentieth Century Interpretations of Light in August.* Englewood Cliffs, N.J.: Prentice-Hall, 1969. In its first part, the collection comprises the D. Abel article (see bibliog. chap. 3), R. Chase's chapter on *Light in August* from his book *The American Novel and Its Tradition* (different from his 1948 article: see bibliog. chaps. 5 and 6), and the three chapters on *Light in August* from their respective books—among the very best on Faulkner—by O. W. Vickery, C. Brooks, and M. Millgate (all three are commented on in the bibliography of the present study). Unfortunately, as is the habit in this series, the essays are generally abridged. Part Two, "View Points," consists of brief extracts of articles and studies giving different opinions about several problems and characters: the unity of the work, Protestantism, sex and women, Joe Christmas, Lena Grove and Byron Bunch, Hightower. The B. McElderry article (see bibliog. chap. 2) comes as an appenxix. D. Minter's introduction is very creditable, especially on the ambivalence of Christmas, divided between the forces of death and those of life.

3. STUDY GUIDES:

None are of any interest: they are summaries of the novel, with occasionally simplistic or even inaccurate comments.

Goethals, Thomas. *Light in August: A Critical Commentary.* New York: American R. D. M. Corporation, 1965.

Juhasz, Leslie A. *William Faulkner's Light in August (A Critical Commentary).* Monarch Notes and Study Guides. New York: Monarch Press, 1965.

Roberts, James L. *Light in August Notes.* Lincoln, Neb.: Cliff's Notes, 1964.

CHAPTER 1

Brown, Calvin S. "Faulkner's Geography and Topography." *PMLA*, 77 (December 1962), pp. 652–59. Provides knowledgeable evidence that the Jefferson of *Light in August* is based on Oxford, Mississippi.

Cullen, John B., with Floyd C. Watkins. *Old Times in the Faulkner Country.* Chapel Hill: University of North Carolina Press, 1961. The frequently spicy reminiscences of an inhabitant of Lafayette County, Miss., who knew Faulkner and hunted with him. Gives numerous possible local—historical and geographical—sources for Faulkner's works.

Kerr, Elizabeth M. *Yoknapatawpha: Faulkner's "Little Postage Stamp of Native Soil."* New York: Fordham University Press, 1969. Superimposes fictional Yoknapatawpha County on actual Lafayette County in Mississippi, with numerous references to *Light in August.* Too dogmatic.

Rubin, Louis D., Jr. "Notes on a Rear-Guard Action." In Frank E. Vandiver, ed., *The Idea of the South.* Chicago: University of Chicago Press, 1964, pp. 27-41. A few comments on the South of Faulkner's works.

CHAPTER 2

Adams, Richard P. *Faulkner: Myth and Motion.* Princeton, N.J.: Princeton University Press, 1968, pp. 84-95. Lena and Joe have a meaning only if they are seen in contrast to each other, and in the context of myths which broaden their significance. The tension between movement and suspension, seen first through Joe and Lena, then, strangely, through Byron and the three main characters.

Baldanza, Frank. "The Structure of *Light in August.*" *Modern Fiction Studies,* 12 (Spring 1967), pp. 67–78. A catalogue both extravagant (the author makes many unjustified analogies) and incomplete (hardly goes beyond the factual level) of what he calls "theme clusters." Restricts himself to their aesthetic and musical value with no conclusion as to their ultimate meaning.

Benson, Carl. "Thematic Design in *Light in August.*" *South Atlantic Quarterly,* 53 (Oct. 1954), pp. 540-55. Relates the novel's structure to the moral conflicts (between self-assertion of the individual and commitment to the community and mankind): Hightower is the moral protagonist. A very good article.

Brooks, Cleanth. *William Faulkner: The Yoknapatawpha Country.* New Haven, Conn.: Yale University Press, 1963, pp. 47-74, 375-81. Studies the individual characters in relation to the community which, for the author, stands as the norm and gives the novel its unity. A very reliable chapter, as is the rest of the book.

Brylowski, Walter. *Faulkner's Olympian Laugh: Myth in the Novels.* Detroit: Wayne State University Press, 1968, pp. 102-17. *Light in August* is the successful juxtaposition of two opposed worlds. Faulkner's is a dual conception of the world. But Hightower is all but ignored.

Hirshleifer, Phyllis. "As Whirlwinds in the South: An Analysis of *Light in August.*" *Perspective,* 2 (Summer 1949), pp. 225-38. Clear but concise study of several aspects of the novel, especially its thematic structure. A good article, which has probably influenced several others.

Howe, Irving. *William Faulkner: A Critical Study.* Second edition, revised and expanded. New York: Vintage Books, 1962, pp. 61-70, 200-14. Interesting remarks. The author criticizes the novel's lack of unity ("a triad of actions") and the disparity between the physical presence of Lena and Hightower and their symbolic function.

McCamy, Edward. "Byron Bunch." *Shenandoah,* 3 (Spring 1952), pp. 8-12. Underlines with precision Byron's role in the book.

McElderry, B. R., Jr. "The Narrative Structure of *Light in August.*" *College English,* 19 (Feb. 1958), pp. 200-207. In spite of the title, only a summary of the novel.

Meats, Stephen E. "Who Killed Joanna Burden?" *Mississippi Quarterly,* 24 (Summer 1971), pp. 271-77. As "there is no positive evidence in the novel to indicate who actually commits the murder," Meats suggests that, as a revenge of a sort against Christmas, Brown might have slashed the throat of Joanna, knocked out by Christmas after she had threatened him with a pistol. This ingenious theory, based on Christmas's apparent right-handedness, is just a tenuous surmise, however, running counter to the gist of the novel.

Millgate, Michael. *The Achievement of William Faulkner.* New York: Random House, 1966. The chapter entitled "The Career" (pp. 1–57) is the best biography of Faulkner so far. (A biographical study by Joseph Blotner is forthcoming.) The chapter on *Light in August* (pp. 124-37) is a stimulating study of the thematic and ironical relationships between the three centers of interest and of the mythical connotations surrounding the characters.

Nash, H. C. "Faulkner's 'Furniture Repairer and Dealer': Knitting up *Light in August.*" *Modern Fiction Studies,* 16 (Winter 1970-71), pp. 529-31. The furniture dealer and his wife bring back warmth and "sentiment" into the novel, and help restore natural continuity. They give the Lena-Byron couple its full significance. Brief but useful comments.

Neufeldt, Leonard. "Time and Man's Possibilities in *Light in August.*" *Georgia Review,* 25 (Spring 1971), pp. 27-40. Except for Lena, who lives in a duration "constant with the temporal rhythm of her environment," all the characters "betray a pathological awareness of time": Byron has become a human watch until he partakes of Lena's rhythm, Hightower is caught up in his past until he returns to life, Joanna is haunted by her past, from which she tries to escape through Joe, and Christmas is "destroyed by time because he expends his time struggling against it." The article also sketchily underlines some resemblances between Joe and Lena.

Tuck, Dorothy. "The Inwardness of the Understanding." In John Unterecker, ed., *Approaches to the Twentieth-Century Novel.* New York: Thomas Y. Crowell, 1965, pp. 79-107. A thorough study of the significance of the characters in relation to each other: the structure is therefore thematic. Points out the detective-story elements in the novel.

Williams, John C. " 'The Final Copper Light of Afternoon': Hightower's Redemption." *Twentieth Century Literature,* 13 (January 1968), pp. 205-15. Shows the progressive changes in Hightower and his redemption, which consists of his acceptance of guilt and reintegration into the human community. Attentive reading of the text, sometimes paraphrased, but does not allow for the ambiguity of the character.

CHAPTER 3

Abel, Darrel. "Frozen Movement in *Light in August.*" *Boston University Studies in English,* 3 (Spring 1957), pp. 32-44. Faulkner sees life as a duration, reality as a flux. To give them a literary form he suspends movement and makes use of symbols (urn, etc.). Interesting references to Bergson (*The Creative Mind*).

Asals, Frederick. "Faulkner's *Light in August.*" *Explicator,* 26 (May 1968), item 74. Draws interesting, albeit somewhat farfetched, parallels between Joe's affair with Joanna and the temptation of Christ.

Holman, C. Hugh. "The Unity of Faulkner's *Light in August.*" *PMLA,* 73 (March 1958), pp. 155-66. The best article on the Christian symbolism in *Light in August,* which the author sees as the only element able to give the novel its unity.

Kimmey, John L. "The Good Earth in *Light in August.*" *Mississippi Quarterly,* 17 (Winter 1963-1964), pp. 1-8. Methodical analysis of each character in relation to nature, immemorial earth. No definite conclusions drawn.

Morrison, Sister Kristin. "Faulkner's Joe Christmas: Character Through Voice." *Texas Studies in Literature and Language,* 2 (Winter 1961), pp. 419-43. The traditional concept of point of view does not work with this novel and should be replaced by the notion of voice, here studied particularly in the first chapters of the novel. Good, thorough article.

Moseley, Edwin M. *Pseudonyms of Christ in the Modern Novel: Motifs and Methods.* Pittsburgh: University of Pittsburgh Press, 1962, pp. 135-51. Study of the characters in the light of Christian symbolism. Sees Joe as more of an image of Christ than a parody.

Pearson, Norman Holmes. "Lena Grove." *Shenandoah,* 3 (Spring 1952), pp. 3-7. A good study. Interesting references to Keats and the "Ode on a Grecian Urn."

Slatoff, Walter J. *Quest for Failure: A Study of William Faulkner.* Ithaca, N.Y.: Cornell University Press, 1960, pp. 173-98 and passim. Characters and themes remain unresolved, ambiguous. The characteristic form of Faulkner's thought is the oxymoron. A few interesting points, but too preoccupied with proving Slatoff's thesis.

CHAPTER 4

Bleikasten, André. "L'espace dans *Lumière d'août.*" *Bulletin de la Faculté des Lettres de Strasbourg,* 46 (Dec. 1967), pp. 406-20. Faulkner links space to consciousness, places to people: the road to Lena, the street to Christmas, the house to Joanna, the window to Hightower. Very good article (in French).

CHAPTER 5

Asselineau, Roger. "Faulkner, moraliste puritain." In *William Faulkner: Configuration critique, La Revue des Lettres Modernes,*

5 (Winter 1958-1959), pp. 231-49. Good article, especially on sexuality, fatality, and liberty. Faulkner seen as a Christian Stoic: endurance is the supreme virtue (in French).

Backman, Melvin. *Faulkner: The Major Years. A Critical Study.* Bloomington: Indiana University Press, 1966, pp. 67-87. The emphasis is the reverse of that of Cleanth Brooks (see bibliog. chap. 2): Backman stresses the isolation and alienation of the individual. Even though most of the chapter is little more than a paraphrase of the novel, the last pages on Christmas are creditable. But Lena's significance and the import of the first and last chapters in the novel are overlooked.

Barth, J. Robert. "Faulkner and the Calvinist Tradition." *Thought,* 39 (Spring 1964), pp. 100-20. Traces the development of the two elements of the Puritan tradition back to Calvin and Luther. Like Hawthorne and Melville, Faulkner stands within the orthodox Calvinist tradition. The concern with evil or corruption and with doom or the "curse" is examined through his major novels (yet Faulkner is not interested in the relationship between man and God implied in the "curse," but in the human situation itself). Useful, though necessarily sketchy.

Berland, Alwyn. "*Light in August:* The Calvinism of William Faulkner." *Modern Fiction Studies,* 8 (Summer 1962), pp. 159-70. *Light in August* as a condemnation of Calvinism because of its intransigence, and a sign of its persistence in the way of thinking and the obsessions of some characters, especially Christmas.

Bowden, Edwin T. *The Dungeon of the Heart: Human Isolation and the American Novel.* New York: Macmillan, 1961, pp. 124-38. Man only escapes from loneliness by self-forgetfulness, sympathy, love. Mediocre analysis, a lot of paraphrasing.

Brooks, Cleanth. See bibliog. chap. 2.

Cabau, Jacques. *La Prairie perdue: Histoire du roman américain.* Paris: Editions du Seuil, 1966, pp. 214-36. This chapter is little more than an introduction to Faulkner and *Light in August* for the general public. It is a series of trenchant comments, often more sonorous than profound, and in spite of some accurate points, it offers a simplified and superficial view of the novel and of its author (in French).

Chase, Richard. *The American Novel and Its Tradition.* Garden City, N.Y.: Doubleday Anchor Books, 1957, pp. 210-19. Interesting chapter, though several debatable points. Joe is not a tragic hero (naturalistic conception of fatality). Hightower is the most successfully drawn character in the book.

Douglas, Harold J., and Robert Daniel. "Faulkner and the Puritanism of the South." *Tennessee Studies in Literature,* 2 (1957), pp. 1-13. "Faulkner's relation to Calvinism resembles that of Joe Christmas in *Light in August,* who detests his stern Presbyterian stepfather, yet prefers his harsh morality to Mrs. McEachern's softness and weakness." The (not new) idea is interesting, but apart from a discussion of the similarities between *The Scarlet Letter* and *As I Lay Dying,* the article remains unsystematic and superficial.

Greer, Scott. "Joe Christmas and the 'Social Self'." *Mississippi Quarterly,* 11 (Fall 1958), pp. 160-66. A sociological analysis of the novel as an exploration of the meaning of race identification in a small Southern town. This article is part of a not particularly distinguished *Mississippi Quarterly* special number on *Light in August.*

Jacobs, Robert D. "William Faulkner: The Passion and the Penance." In Louis D. Rubin, Jr., and Robert C. Jacobs, eds. *South: Modern Southern Literature in Its Cultural Setting.* Garden City, N.Y.: Doubleday Dolphin Books, 1961, pp. 142-76 (on *Light in August,* pp. 157-63). In contrast to R. Chase, sees Christmas as a tragic hero, not totally a victim of heredity and environment.

Kazin, Alfred. "The Stillness of *Light in August.*" *Partisan Review,* 24 (Autumn 1957), pp. 519-38. Long article, frequently quoted: underlines opposition between Lena (country, life . . .) and Christmas (town, rejection of life . . .). Sensible remarks on Joe's alienation, symbolic of the condition of modern man, translated by the distance at which the character seems to appear.

Lind, Ilse Dusoir. "The Calvinistic Burden of *Light in August.*" *"New England Quarterly,* 30 (Sept. 1957), pp. 307-29. Good study of Joanna and Joe, victims of a Calvinist tradition and education.

Longley, John L., Jr. "Joe Christmas: The Hero in the Modern World." *Virginia Quarterly Review,* 33 (Spring 1957), pp. 233-49. Incorporated into *The Tragic Mask: A Study of Faulkner's Heroes.* Chapel Hill: University of North Carolina Press, 1963. Sees Joe as a tragic hero who retains some freedom of choice. Comparison with Oedipus.

Nilon, Charles H. *Faulkner and the Negro.* New York: Citadel Press, 1965, pp. 73-93. Unfortunately of little interest. Paraphrase, no ideas.

O'Connor, William Van. "Protestantism in Yoknapatawpha County." *Hopkins Review,* 5 (Spring 1952), pp. 26-42. Reprinted in Louis D. Rubin, Jr., and Robert D. Jacobs, eds., *Southern Renascence: The Literature of the Modern South,* Baltimore: Johns Hopkins Press, 1953, pp. 153-69. Revised for *The Tangled Fire of William Faulkner,* Minneapolis: University of Minnesota Press, 1954, pp. 72-87. Sees Protestantism as the central issue of *Light in August.* A few, too brief remarks on the ambivalent view of religion as both destructive (the church is one of the agents of Christmas's destruction) and humane (Byron Bunch). But mostly a paraphrase of the novel.

Pearce, Richard. "Faulkner's One Ring Circus." *Wisconsin Studies in Contemporary Literature,* 7 (Fall 1966), pp. 270-83. Disputable but stimulating article. Sees *Light in August* as an essentially comic novel: tragic characters become grotesque as they struggle with forces beyond their comprehension (image of the chessboard).

Sandstrom, Glenn. "Identity Diffusion: Joe Christmas and Quentin Compson." *American Quarterly,* 19 (Summer 1967), pp. 207-23. These two characters are examined in the light of psychoanalyst Eric H. Erikson's theory of identity. "Without benefit of Freud, as he claimed, Faulkner captured and ordered . . . some problems of identity that psychologists began to itemize and analyze only a generation later."

Vickery, Olga W. *The Novels of William Faulkner: A Critical Interpretation.* Revised edition. Baton Rouge: Louisiana State University Press, 1964, pp. 66-83. Novel seen in the light of the conflict between the private and public images of each character. Excellent interpretation, perhaps too coherent.

Volpe, Edmond L. *A Reader's Guide to William Faulkner.* New York: Farrar, Straus & Co., 1964, pp. 151-74. Sound study of the themes in relation to each character. Hightower remains locked in his past.

Waggoner, Hyatt H. *William Faulkner: From Jefferson to the World.* Lexington: University of Kentucky Press, 1959, pp. 100-20. Christmas and Lena represent two opposed concepts of mankind. Lena has the last word, but less weight. Sound remarks on the moral ambiguities and aesthetic failings of the novel.

Weisberger, Jean. *Faulkner et Dostoievski: Confluences et influences.* Brussels: Presses Universitaires de Bruxelles, 1968, pp. 175-88. Views Christmas as a scapegoat for the sins of society. A stimulating comparison with Raskolnikov, who, unlike Christmas, initially enjoys some freedom of choice. Yet tends to make Faulkner more Dostoevskian than he is (there seem to be confluences much more than precise influences). In French.

———. "Faulkner's Monomaniacs: Their Indebtedness to Raskolnikov." *Comparative Literature Studies,* 5 (June 1968), pp. 181-93. A comparison of Christmas and several of Faulkner's major characters with Raskolnikov.

Yorks, Samuel A. "Faulkner's Woman: The Peril of Mankind." *Arizona Quarterly,* 17 (Summer 1961), pp. 119-29. Good article on paradoxical conception of Woman in Faulkner's novels.

Zink, Karl E. "Faulkner's Garden: Woman and the Immemorial Earth," *Modern Fiction Studies,* 2 (Autumn 1956), pp. 139-49. Very good article on Faulkner's women (identified with the fecund earth). Men's frequent hostility towards them.

CHAPTER 6

Beck, Warren. "William Faulkner's Style." *American Prefaces,* 6 (Spring 1941), pp. 195-211. Quoted from Frederick J. Hoffman and Olga Vickery, eds., *William Faulkner: Three Decades of Criticism.* East Lansing: Michigan State University Press, 1960, pp. 142-56. Very good article on Faulkner's two kinds of style, which are in fact often mingled since Faulkner disregards the demands of both objectivity and verisimilitude. Synthesis of modern narrative methods and a poetic, interpretative use of language.

Chase, Richard. "The Stone and the Crucifixion: Faulkner's *Light in August.*" *Kenyon Review,* 10 (Autumn 1948), pp. 539-51. Rather abstract remarks on the symbolism of the circle (conscience, culture, tradition) and the straight line (modernism, alienation): the novel is "a poetry of physics."

Hopper, Vincent F. "Faulkner's Paradise Lost." *Virginia Quarterly Review,* 23 (Summer 1947), pp. 405-20. General article; among other things, stresses that Faulkner's symbols operate on the emotional not the intellectual level. Comments on the direct, physical effect of his art.

Larsen, Eric. "The Barrier of Language: The Irony of Language in Faulkner." *Modern Fiction Studies,* 13 (Spring 1967), pp. 19-31. Language alone cannot communicate experience; it is an experience in itself. Similar conclusions to those of Walter J. Slatoff (see bibliog. chap. 3).

Leaver, Florence. "Faulkner: The Word as Principle and Power." *South Atlantic Quarterly,* 57 (Autumn 1958), pp. 464-76. Quoted from *Three Decades of Criticism* (see bibliog. chap. 7), pp. 199-209. Catalogues some of the techniques of Faulkner's style: use of abstract and negative words, creation of the compound words, repetition of certain words.

Morris, Wright. "The Violent Land: Some Observations on the Faulkner Country." *Magazine of Art,* 45 (March 1952), pp. 99-103. Some excellent remarks on Faulkner's expressionism.

Zink, Karl E. "William Faulkner: Form as Experience." *South Atlantic Quarterly,* 53 (July 1954), pp. 384-403. Stimulating appraisal of Faulkner's "technique of accretion," the continuity of his style, which transcends the sentence form in his ample prose, his immediacy in the simple direct prose.

CHAPTER 7

Hoffman, Frederick J., and Olga W. Vickery, eds. *William Faulkner: Three Decades of Criticism.* East Lansing: Michigan State University Press, 1960. "An Introduction," by F. J. Hoffman, pp. 1-50.

Price-Stephens, Gordon. "The British Reception of William Faulkner, 1929-1962." *Mississippi Quarterly,* 17 (Summer 1964), pp. 119-200.

Woodworth, Stanley D. *William Faulkner en France (1931-1952).* Paris, M. J. Minard, 1959. In French.

These three items provide useful information on the critical reception of Faulkner in the United States, Great Britain, and France. For the interpretations of *Light in August,* see the text and notes of this chapter.

Index